Palgrave Studies in Animals and Literature

Series Editors
Susan McHugh
Department of English
University of New England
Auburn, USA

Robert McKay
School of English
University of Sheffield
Sheffield, UK

John Miller
School of English
University of Sheffield
Sheffield, UK

Various academic disciplines can now be found in the process of executing an 'animal turn', questioning the ethical and philosophical grounds of human exceptionalism by taking seriously the nonhuman animal presences that haunt the margins of history, anthropology, philosophy, sociology and literary studies. Such work is characterised by a series of broad, cross-disciplinary questions. How might we rethink and problematise the separation of the human from other animals? What are the ethical and political stakes of our relationships with other species? How might we locate and understand the agency of animals in human cultures?

This series publishes work that looks, specifically, at the implications of the 'animal turn' for the field of English Studies. Language is often thought of as the key marker of humanity's difference from other species; animals may have codes, calls or songs, but humans have a mode of communication of a wholly other order. The primary motivation is to muddy this assumption and to animalise the canons of English Literature by rethinking representations of animals and interspecies encounter. Whereas animals are conventionally read as objects of fable, allegory or metaphor (and as signs of specifically human concerns), this series significantly extends the new insights of interdisciplinary animal studies by tracing the engagement of such figuration with the material lives of animals. It examines textual cultures as variously embodying a debt to or an intimacy with animals and advances understanding of how the aesthetic engagements of literary arts have always done more than simply illustrate natural history. We publish studies of the representation of animals in literary texts from the Middle Ages to the present and with reference to the discipline's key thematic concerns, genres and critical methods. The series focuses on literary prose and poetry, while also accommodating related discussion of the full range of materials and texts and contexts (from theatre and film to fine art, journalism, the law, popular writing and other cultural ephemera) with which English studies now engages.

Series Board:
Karl Steel (Brooklyn College)
Erica Fudge (Strathclyde)
Kevin Hutchings (UNBC)
Philip Armstrong (Canterbury)
Carrie Rohman (Lafayette)
Wendy Woodward (Western Cape)

Robert A. Kitchen • Glenn Peers

The Bird Who Sang the Trisagion of Isaac of Antioch

Becoming Parrot in a Late Antique Syriac Sermon

Robert A. Kitchen
Regina, SK, Canada

Glenn Peers
Bennington, VT, USA

ISSN 2634-6338   ISSN 2634-6346 (electronic)
Palgrave Studies in Animals and Literature
ISBN 978-3-031-60076-0   ISBN 978-3-031-60077-7 (eBook)
https://doi.org/10.1007/978-3-031-60077-7

© The Editor(s) (if applicable) and The Author(s), under exclusive license to Springer Nature Switzerland AG 2024

This work is subject to copyright. All rights are solely and exclusively licensed by the Publisher, whether the whole or part of the material is concerned, specifically the rights of translation, reprinting, reuse of illustrations, recitation, broadcasting, reproduction on microfilms or in any other physical way, and transmission or information storage and retrieval, electronic adaptation, computer software, or by similar or dissimilar methodology now known or hereafter developed.

The use of general descriptive names, registered names, trademarks, service marks, etc. in this publication does not imply, even in the absence of a specific statement, that such names are exempt from the relevant protective laws and regulations and therefore free for general use.

The publisher, the authors and the editors are safe to assume that the advice and information in this book are believed to be true and accurate at the date of publication. Neither the publisher nor the authors or the editors give a warranty, expressed or implied, with respect to the material contained herein or for any errors or omissions that may have been made. The publisher remains neutral with regard to jurisdictional claims in published maps and institutional affiliations.

Cover illustration: Pattern © Melisa Hasan

This Palgrave Macmillan imprint is published by the registered company Springer Nature Switzerland AG.
The registered company address is: Gewerbestrasse 11, 6330 Cham, Switzerland

Paper in this product is recyclable.

Preface

This book is the first English-language study of one of the most important and prolific theologians of the Syriac Church, Isaac of Antioch, who was active in the second half of the fifth century. To be fair, his corpus is still uncertain, and biographical details are scant; study of this writer is still in early stages. But Isaac was a highly original thinker, and his arguments and ideas deserve careful and sympathetic examination. This book focuses on Isaac's most renowned, but little studied, sung metrical homily, a homily about a theological parrot: "On the Bird Who Sang the Trisagion." We offer here a wide-ranging study of the homily, including theological and historical analyses, and a complete translation of the text. This little-known text is a noteworthy addition to Patristic Studies, and it has no precise match in the literature.

While the heart of the book is the translation of the homily, we also intend to bring this sophisticated text into conversation with current scholarly debates in the fields of animal studies, performance studies, and media studies. For we argue that the homily puts a parrot in the position of righteous protagonist, who not only resolves a highly contentious contemporary conflict over liturgical form, but who also provides the subject position that Isaac emulates and occupies. Isaac becomes parrot, as parrot becomes human. In that new subject-becoming, Isaac sings for new models of knowing God.

This brief overview already indicates the diverse approaches adopted within this book. In the first place, Isaac is that kind of thinker—sophisticated, challenging, imaginative, idiosyncratic. His writing invites (if not demands) intensive engagement. In the second, basic facts are unresolved: Isaac's corpus, his vita, milieu, all need painstaking work still. In the third, Isaac's work deserves to be read by contemporary readers of every variety. Different methods work best to bring out the multifaceted complexity of his writing and to reach the largest possible audience.

This collaboration has been deeply stimulating and fruitful. Robert Kitchen's specialty is Syriac language and the history and theology of the Syriac Church, and his first responsibility was significant, to provide a clear and readable translation of Isaac's sermon. The second was to provide a concise and lucid account of Isaac's oeuvre, career, and the historical and theological contexts in which this sermon was written and performed. This account is the Introduction. In the Interpretative Essay following the translation, Glenn Peers provides an extended analysis of Isaac's sermon in the context of humans' long and complicated history of interactions with parrots and other birds capable of speech. Like so many writers, Isaac shapes his sense of self in relation to his revelatory parrot, and he moves in and out of an affirmation of the bird's agency, will, and mind. This is not surprising, given the various ways across centuries that parrots have troubled categories that humans have long considered exclusively their own—speech, mind, and autonomy that define and distinguish the human in contrast to the larger, lesser category of non-human animal. Isaac productively engages these apparently modern concerns, and in this book, we can approach his words, not only within his immediate historical context, but also as he participates in a long history of how parrots show us what we humans are (and are promised by God).

A note about pronouns: we have decided to take divergent approaches concerning the pronoun used for the bird. In Syriac, all animals are feminine in form. We decided that in the Introduction and Translation the pronouns it/its would apply, bowing to some conventions around animals and language usage. (For clarity, he/him/his is used for Jesus and Satan.) However, in the Interpretative Essay, the choice was made to use they/their/theirs. Parrots are a monomorphic creature, meaning it is very difficult to tell their gender, except with DNA testing. Yet parrots, of course, recognize gender and mate mostly for life. As explained in a note in that last section of the book, the birds might even be considered queer (they were deeply fascinating to Andy Warhol for this reason), and the diachronic approach followed in this Essay, moreover, makes 'they' defensible and arguably more authentic to Isaac's open vision of human-parrot.

Regina, SK, Canada Robert A. Kitchen
Bennington, VT, USA Glenn Peers

ACKNOWLEDGEMENTS

(GP) I'd like to thank Adam Becker for his collegial generosity; Przemyslaw Marciniak, Tristan Schmidt, and Katarzyna Piotrowska, at the University of Silesia in Katowice, who offered me a stimulating forum for presenting some of these ideas and arguments; and Marco Formisano, who gave helpful advice. And always Virginia Burrus.

Finally, I want to call out Julie and the best parrot-person I know, Shannon Steiner.

Praise for The Bird Who Sang the Trisagion *of Isaac of Antioch*

"Birds can play an important role in literature; situated in time between Aristophanes' *Birds* and Farid al-Din 'Attar's *Conference of the Birds*, Isaac of Antioch's poem on the bird who sang the Trisagion plays its part in theological controversy of the time. Robert Kitchen introduces the context and provides the poem with its first English translation, while Glenn Peers explores the parrot's role in the wider context of humanity's fascination with parrots. Clearly a must for all parrot-lovers."
—Sebastian Brock, Fellow of the British Academy, *Emeritus Reader in Syriac Studies and Emeritus Fellow of Wolfson College, Oxford, UK*

"In this polished volume, the authors show Isaac's homily on the parrot to be a sophisticated, multilayered text that will appeal both to scholars of Christian antiquity as well as to contemporary readers, especially those interested in animal studies."
—Patricia Cox Miller, *The Bishop W. Earl Ledden Professor of Religion, Emerita, Syracuse University, USA*

"Isaac of Antioch is a mysterious figure of late antique Syriac Christianity, prolific yet understudied. Robert Kitchen's clear introduction is followed by his elegant translation of Isaac's surprising and revelatory encounter with a parrot, an unlikely source of fresh theological, exegetical, and liturgical wonder for Isaac's poetic exploration. Glenn Peers adds an interpretive essay that reflects on the significance of non-human beings for ancient Christians and ourselves, refracted through a remarkable tour of the relationship between humans and parrots across vast swaths of history, past and present. There is much to learn here, and much to enjoy—whether of Isaac's world or our own. Partnering meticulous scholarship with imaginative insight and depth, this is work that instructs and delights at every turn."
—Susan Ashbrook Harvey, *Willard Prescott and Annie McClelland Smith Professor of History and Religion, Brown University, USA*

"In an age where the parrot is often reduced to the symbol of mindless repetition—parroting—or merely seen as a colorful pet, the authors offer a captivating account of a parrot that transcended these clichés. Isaac's parrot is not only capable

of speaking but defies conventional expectations of the human-animal relationship by helping a human understand a theological truth. This book seamlessly blends solid philological work, an enjoyable translation of a challenging text, with a brilliant interpretation of the Syriac mēmrā. After more than 1500 years Robert Kitchen and Glenn Peers return the parrot its voice."
—Przemysław Marciniak, *University of Silesia in Katowice, Poland*

"Could a bird be a theological teacher? Indeed, it was a parrot that inspired a key text on the Christological debates in late 5th-century Antioch. In their translation and analysis of Isaac of Antioch's *Mēmrā* about 'The Bird Who Sang the Trisagion,' Robert Kitchen and Glenn Peers masterfully combine theological and historical analysis with historical human-animal studies. Their highly original perspective on animal (parrot) agency and human 'parroting' demonstrates how even a seemingly anthropocentric activity, such as the exploration for the true faith, can be read as a multi-species event."
—Tristan Schmidt, *Uniwersytet Śląski w Katowicach, Poland*

CONTENTS

1 A Fowl Theology of the Cross: Isaac of Antioch's *Mēmrā* on the Parrot   1

2 Translation: Isaac of Antioch's Mēmrā on the Parrot   25

3 Interpretative Essay: Becoming Parrot—Voice's Subject Formation   63

Select Bibliography   119

Index   125

CHAPTER 1

A Fowl Theology of the Cross: Isaac of Antioch's *Mēmrā* on the Parrot

Abstract This chapter introduces the shadowy figure of Isaac of Antioch, a prolific but understudied Syriac writer of the latter part of the fifth century. It provides context for the focus of the book, the verse sermon (or *memra*) Isaac composed after he encountered a parrot who revealed to him the correct position in what became known as the Addition controversy. In the 480s, the divisive patriarch of Antioch, Peter the Fuller, attempted to introduce a clause into the Trisagion prayer, and his innovation caused major ruptures among differently aligned Christians in his see and beyond. We have few details about the events and figures of the controversy, and Isaac's sermon provides vital clues about that historical moment and about human-animal relationships to God.

Keywords Isaac of Antioch • Addition controversy • Peter the Fuller • Syriac Christianity • Parrots • Animal Studies

PARROTS AND DOVES

Animals have always confounded our human assumption of superiority, and indeed human priority to salvation, according to Christian beliefs. Many theologians over the past two millennia have explored these understandings of human-animal distinctions and human claims to exclusive

© The Author(s), under exclusive license to Springer Nature Switzerland AG 2024
R. A. Kitchen, G. Peers, *The Bird Who Sang the Trisagion of Isaac of Antioch*, Palgrave Studies in Animals and Literature,
https://doi.org/10.1007/978-3-031-60077-7_1

entry into heaven.[1] This study examines one particular theological analysis of the possibility of animals sharing salvation and even of their greater proximity to the Lord. In the 480s, in the cosmopolitan city of Antioch, a Syriac churchman of great eloquence and intelligence—Isaac—witnessed the vocal profession of the true faith by a small bird, a parrot. Isaac wrote a lengthy verse sermon, a *mēmrā*, concerning this transformative experience. He was never the same, and he wanted his audiences to hear, too, that this parrot was a superior creature who recognized God's will better than the clamorous press of humans around them in that church square in Antioch.

The identification of Isaac's interlocutor has traditionally been a parrot. Isaac uses a less specific word, *parahtha* (ܦܪܚܬܐ), which covers birds generally, and in fact there is no specific term for parrot in Syriac, but the tenth-century *Chronica Minora* uses *pastiaqos* (ܦܣܛܝܐܩܘܣ), probably a loan word from the Greek Ψιττακός (Greek also had παπαγάλος for this bird). The second volume of the *Chronica Minora* records the incident in Antioch in which Isaac of Antioch saw the bird and then wrote his *mēmrā*,

> But after a while the tyrant Basilikos was killed and Zeno again took control of the kingdom. In those times, the School of the Persians was abolished.[2] And during that period when Peter the Fuller was leading the Church of Antioch, Mar Isaac, the writer from Edessa, went down to Antioch. He saw a bird, which is called *pastiaqos*, shouting that hymn of Three Times Holy (Trisagion) and that He was crucified. [The bird] shamed the heretics, and Isaac wrote a *mēmrā* in the Aramaic (Syriac) language concerning this.[3]

In terms of historical criticism, it may be a matter of the chicken or the egg, for the chronicle entry is based on Isaac's homily, not on an independent source. Was the parrot a trope, or did Isaac really witness a bird sing?

---

[1] A noteworthy, recent work on the subject is Christina Nellist, *Eastern Orthodox Christianity and Animal Suffering: Ancient Voices in Modern Theology* (Cambridge: Cambridge Scholars Publishing, 2018).

[2] The School of the Persians, or the School of Edessa, was an intellectual center for education and translation in the mid-fifth century, mostly of Nestorian authors. It was closed in 489 by Emperor Zeno for its Nestorian tendencies, and many members migrated into the Persian Empire and established the School of Nisibis.

[3] *Chronica Minora*, ed. Ernest W. Brooks, Corpus Scriptorum Christianorum Orientalium, vol. 3, Scriptores Syri, vol. 3 (Louvain: E. Typographeo Reipublicae, 1904), II: 217.3–11.

With some qualifications expressed below, we are taking Isaac at his word that there was such a revelatory bird, and indeed that it did give him an insightful and transformative figure by which to teach the Orthodox faith. We also follow the *Chronica Minora*, then, in settling upon the identification of the bird as parrot, which by far makes the most sense of Isaac's description of and claims for the bird he witnessed.[4]

Isaac is creative with the language he used to describe the parrot's communication. The Syriac verb Isaac employed is *l'ēz* (ܠܥܙ), which can be rendered 'singing' or 'chirping' or 'squawking.' Birds sing, but so do we; birds 'chirp'—maybe too trivial a choice for this bird; and 'squawk' is what parrots do, but it falls on the heavy side for theological profundity. All three will be used. Moreover, all these translations will be employed for human speech here, because Isaac's argument rests in part on the equal spread of voices among humans, animals, and things in his *mēmrā*.[5] In his powerfully evoked world of sound, Isaac uses this verb to spread speech and voice across many entities (again, human, animal, and thing), and while 'chirp' may appear out of place for a deeply serious theological work, it demonstrates Isaac's capacious hearing, which is open to all sources of communication from the Lord.

Isaac's encounter and his decision to write such a long meditation on it are striking in the context not only of the theological controversy roiling Antioch in the 480s, but also of birds' possible contentiousness in the Miaphysite church. It is worth noting that, upon entering his newly appointed episcopal see in Mabbug (also known as Hierapolis), Philoxenos quickly discovered that the dove, as the icon of the Holy Spirit, was already entrenched in the 'Holy City.' It had long been the sacred bird of the Syrian goddess Atargatis and been taken on by Christians to stand for the third element of the Trinity. Reacting strongly (and typically) to that syncretism, Philoxenos forbade the use of these eucharistic doves.[6] This proscription was in 485, so perhaps he had in mind another bird to come off the bench and proclaim the Orthodox faith, Isaac's parrot who sang the

---

[4] Another humorous anecdote features a bird (*pārahthā*), most readers would assume is a parrot, "A Feathered Thing Happened on the Way to the Agora: A Syriac Variant of the Ancient Greek Sphinx Story" [Cambridge Add. MS 2023, folio 48a, trans. Simon Samuel Ford and Kirsty Stewart (forthcoming)].

[5] Strong precedent exists for humans being given animal voices. See, for example, *Iliad* 3.151–2, where the Trojan elders have the delicate voices of cicadas in a tree.

[6] André de Halleux, *Philoxène de Mabbog: Sa vie, ses écrits, sa théologie* (Louvain: Imprimerie orientaliste, 1963), 89–90.

Trisagion and its Addition in Antioch. But it might also reveal a faultline in contemporary culture where animals were subjects of particularly intense focus, both positive (Isaac) and negative (Philoxenos).[7]

WHICH ISAAC?

The identity of the writer we call Isaac of Antioch is still an open question.[8] We know almost nothing about his life or his spheres of activity, and his corpus is unresolved. Even in Late Antiquity, there was some confusion over this writer. In a letter to his contemporary, John of Litarba (or Litharb), Jacob of Edessa (d. 708) recognized that three authors might be identified as the author of our *mēmrā*.[9] Isaac of Amid, who flourished in the late fourth century, is remembered by Jacob as a student of Zenobius and a pupil of Ephrem, who moved from Amid (Diyarbakır) to Rome and Constantinople. He is said to have written two *mēmrē*, on the secular games in Rome, and on the fall of Rome to Alaric in 410, but both works are lost. Another shadowy figure is Isaac of Edessa, a Miaphysite priest in Edessa during the first quarter of the sixth century. *Mēmrē* attributed to him supported both the Chalcedonian and Miaphysite positions, dependent on whether these were written before or after his conversion to the latter confession.

The third candidate is most plausibly the author here. Jacob identified another Isaac as a resident of Edessa, who had moved to Antioch ca. 474–91 and supported Patriarch Peter the Fuller during the Trisagion controversy (484–5). The concerns expressed in the *mèmrā* on the parrot arose during this period, in which champions of the Miaphysite confession vied with supporters of Chalcedonian christology. This same figure is the

---

[7] On this question for the period under discussion more broadly, see the important work of Patricia Cox Miller, *In the Eye of the Animal: Zoological Imagination in Ancient Christianity* (Philadelphia: University of Pennsylvania Press, 2018).

[8] The forthcoming book by Adam Becker will certainly advance many of these questions of identity, attributions, and historical context, even while they are not answered in this book—it remains a vexed question, despite the groundbreaking work done in that forthcoming study.

[9] *A Letter from Jacob of Edessa to John the Stylite of Litarba Concerning Ecclesiastical Canons: Edited from Ms. Br. Mus. Add. 14,493 with Introduction, Translation and Commentary*, ed. and trans. Karl-Erik Rignell (Lund: CWK Gleerup, 1979), Letter 14 (British Library, Add. 12,172, f. 123r–v).

principal Isaac of Antioch who authored most of the *mēmrē* that have survived under the name of Isaac.[10] This identification, most commonly held among scholars, is followed in this study.

LITERARY WORKS OF ISAAC OF ANTIOCH

The heyday of theological literature during Late Antiquity (ca. 300–800) occurred around the christological controversies of the councils of Nicea (325) and Chalcedon (451) in all the major languages–Latin, Greek, and Syriac. Its literature rivaled in volume and breadth of subjects the extent of classical Latin and Greek languages.[11] While Syriac was predominantly religious in character, almost completely Christian, historical chronicles and scientific treatises are significant aspects of the Syriac corpus. Syriac continued to be used as a spoken and literary language well into the second millennium, although following the Islamic conquests of the mid-seventh century, Arabic became the primary language of society and commerce.

Arguably the least studied of the major Syriac writers, Isaac of Antioch is one of the most prolific.[12] We know him almost exclusively through his writings. Scholars have identified a basic corpus, but other texts are waiting to be edited and studied. The resource website, *syri.ac*, edited by Scott F. Johnson, Morgan Reed, and Jack Tannous, contains titles and links to 183 *mēmrē*, plus 19 *madrāshē*. Isaac wrote his *mēmrē* in poetic meter. No prose works are extant. Edward G. Mathews, Jr. adds several more *mēmrē* not found in the principal collections of Syriac authors produced by earlier scholars, namely Giuseppe Simone Assemani, T. J. Lamy, Gustavus Bickell,

---

[10] Tanios Bou Mansour, "Une clé pour la distinction des écrits des Isaac d'Antioche," *Ephemerides Theologicae Lovaniensus* 79, no. 4 (2003): 365–402.

[11] Aaron Michael Butts, "The Classical Syriac Language" in *The Syriac World*, ed. Daniel King (London: Routledge, 2019), 222–42.

[12] Isaac remains understudied. He does not figure, for example, in a recent handbook of Syriac studies, with the sole exception of Sebastian P. Brock, "Later Syriac Poetry," in *The Syriac World*, 327–38, here 328. But see now Grigory Kessel, "A Syriac Monk's Reading of Ephrem of Nisibis: A Perspective on Syriac Monastic Miscellanies," in *Florilegia Syriaca: Mapping a Knowledge-Organizing Practice in the Syriac World*, ed. Emiliano Fiori and Bishara Ebeid (Leiden: Brill, 2023), 330–52, here 338–48.

and Paul Bedjan.[13] Only a small number of Isaac's *mēmrē* have been translated: four in English,[14] four in Italian,[15] two in French,[16] and sixteen in German.[17] Largely inaccessible outside the field of experts in Syriac studies, his work is full of interest and of opportunities for future research, for reasons we hope will become clear in the following study and translation.

---

[13] Edward G. Mathews, Jr., "The Works Attributed to Isaac of Antioch: A[nother] Preliminary Checklist," *Hugoye: Journal of Syriac Studies* 6, no. 1 (2004): 51–76.

[14] Cyril Moss, "Isaac of Antioch, Homily on the Royal City," *Zeitschrift für Semitik* 8 (1932): 61–73; Stanley Kazan, "Isaac of Antioch's Homily against the Jews," *Oriens Christianus* 45 (1961): 30–53; "On the End Times" (Vat. Syr. 120: ff. 74r–75v), Digital Humanities in Syriac Studies & Beth Mardutho Syriac II (2019); Robert Kitchen, "On the Vigil which took place in Antioch; and On 'It is Good to Give Thanks to the Lord,'" [= Bedjan 68.815–821], an appendix to Glenn Peers, *Byzantine Media Subjects* (Ithaca: Cornell University Press, 2024), 247–52. Adam Becker's forthcoming study and translation of numerous *mēmrē* will be a significant contribution to the field.

[15] Giuseppe Furlani, "Tre discorsi metrici d'Isacco d'Antiochia sulla fede," *Rivista trimestrale di studi filosofici e religiosi* 4, no. 3 (1923): 257–87 [= Bedjan, 800–804, 789–800, 712–725]; and Giuseppe Furlani, "La psicologia d'Isacco d'Antiochia," *Giornale critico della filosofia italiana* 7 (1926): 241–53 [= Bedjan, 399–408].

[16] Paul Feghali, "Isaac d'Antioche, poème sur l'incarnation du Verbe," *Parole d'Orient* 10 (1981–1982): 79–102 [= Bedjan, 789–800; Bickell I, 2–24]; Paul Feghali, "Isaac d'Antioche, une hymne sur l'Incarnation," *Parole d'Orient* 11 (1983): 201–22 [= Bedjan, 712–725; Bickell I, 54–78].

[17] Gustav Bickell, *Ausgewählte Gedichte der syrischen Kirchenväter, Cyrillonas, Baläus, Isaak v. Antiochien und Jakob v. Sarug, zum ersten Male aus dem Syrischen übersetzt*, Bibliothek der Kirchenväter, vol. 12 (Kempten: Kösel, 1872), 109–91 [Bedjan, 789–800 (=Bickell I.2–24); 712–725 (=Bickell I.54–78); 815–821 (=Bickell I.294–306); 158–170 (=Bickell I.250–274); 171–180 (=Bickell I.274–294)].

P.S. Landersdorfer, *Ausgewählte Gedichte der syrischen Dichter, aus dem Syrischen übersetzt*, Bibliothek der Kirchenväter, vol. 6 (Kempten: Kösel, 1913), 101–248 [Bedjan, 789–800 (=Bickell I.2–24); 805–815 (=Bickell I.32–48); 712–725 (=Bickell I.54–78), 800–804 (=Bickell I.24–32), 621–641 (=Bickell II.236–266); 454–468 (=Bickell I.178–204); 539–566 (=Bickell II.266–352); 815–821 (=Bickell I.294–306); 158–170 (=Bickell I.250–274), 171–180 (=Bickell I.274–294), 145–152,153–158]; and

Paul Krüger, "Der dem Isaac von Antiochien zugeschriebene Sermo über den Glauben," *Ostkirchliche Studien* 1 (1952): 46–54 [= Bedjan, 655–664].

The Mēmrā

Isaac's *Mēmrā* on the parrot is found in a handful of manuscripts that are now available digitally, but no critical edition has yet been attempted.[18] It consists of 1068 lines in 7 + 7 syllabic poetic meter, generally in two-line stanzas as the unit of meaning. A gap of apparently two folios is found in all extant manuscripts. The gap is noted by the scribes, suggesting that this folio was misplaced very early in the transmission progress. It is difficult to be precise about how many lines/stanzas have been lost, but an estimate from several manuscripts suggests 40 to 70 lines are now missing.

Very little scholarly work has been directed at this *mēmrā*. And yet it has a certain renown. As Michel van Esbroeck begins his article on the sermon, "Every student who starts to study Syriac literature is astonished to hear that one of its longest poems was devoted to a parrot able to sing the Trishagion according to the addition of Peter the Fuller."[19] The sermon has always possessed a quality of charming novelty, but perhaps the scale of the work was off-putting for extended study. Bickell originally claimed that the *mēmrā* was the longest such text in Syriac literature, and this is one reason it has acquired a 'niche' notoriety. However, that position has been challenged by van Esbroeck, who accurately asserts that the text comprises a 'mere' 1068 lines of 7+7 syllable hemistichs. Bickell had counted each hemistich and so incorrectly doubled the length of the *mēmrā*. Jacob of Sarug's *mēmrā* on Jonah endures for 2540 lines, and there are others that outlast the parrot *mēmrā*.

van Esbroeck's study stands still as a solid starting point for analysis. Distinctively, van Esbroeck declares his investment in the literary qualities of the sermon and its complex theological positions—such literary appreciation is not so common in Syriac studies. In this brief study, moreover, van Esbroeck covers a good deal of ground: he attempts to set the sermon

---

[18] Two published versions exist, both transcribing British Library Additional 14592, ff. 1r–15v: Gustav Bickell, *S. Isaaci Antiocheni, Doctorus Syrorum, Opera Omni* (Giessen: Sumtibus J. Rickeri, 1877), I: 84–174, non-vocalized Syriac text and Latin translation; Paul Bedjan, *Homiliae S. Isaaci Syri Antiocheni* (Leipzig: Harrassowitz, 1903), 737–88, vocalized Syriac text, no translation.

Four other manuscripts are extant: Harvard 71, ff. 73v–83r; Berlin Staatsbibliothek Ms. Or 941, ff. 257r–269v; Birmingham Mingana Syr. 369, ff. 24v–29v; Birmingham Mingana Syr. 554, ff. 219r–235v.

[19] Michel van Esbroeck, "The Memra on the Parrot by Isaac of Antioch," *Journal of Theological Studies* 47 (1996): 464–76.

into the wider historical and theological debates of the Addition, into the career of Peter the Fuller, and follows some of its doctrinal implications in Orthodox and East Christian milieus. He takes a divergent stance from our own, however, in his undervaluing of Isaac's interrogation of the parrot, who is "no more than a vignette" for van Esbroeck. We examine the *mēmrā* from the perspective of the parrot as a central, determinant actor, and not an anecdotal convenience for the writer.

Moreover, Emidio Vergani has more recently made a substantial study of the *mēmrā*, both as an overview and a detailed study of some of its key elements.[20] He treats the complexity of the manuscript transmission of this text within the uncertain terrain of Isaac's corpus, and he attempts to place the sermon in the dynamic unfolding of events in the eastern church in the 480s, before turning to the rich set of voices Isaac deploys. For the parrot is only one voice among many in the sermon, voices that include human and animal, but also strikingly a wide range of things, like the cross—a symbol of great richness, very much within the Syriac mode, Vergani suggests. And the role of the parrot is given a sympathetic rendering here, though primarily as a charming coda to his erudite discussion.

While many mentions of the sermon on the parrot have accumulated over the years, these studies represent the meager bibliography dedicated to it (however, accomplished the studies indeed are). Building on these few contributions, we provide an exposition of basic features of the text in its original context, as well as a wide-ranging analysis of this sermon in the history of human description and speculation about the species that fascinated Isaac so deeply.

Peter the Fuller and Antioch of the 480s

There are few historical sources for this turbulent period of the church history of Antioch, namely the latter third of the fifth century. Isaac provides precious, if indirect, evidence of the high stakes for theology at the

---

[20] Emidio Vergani, "L'omelia sul pappagallo: l'esegesi in un testo di Isacco di Antiochia," in *La tradizione cristiana Siro-occidentale (V-VII secolo). Atti del 4° Incontro sull'Oriente Cristiano di tradizione siriaca (Milano, Biblioteca Ambrosiana, 13 maggio 2005)*, ed. Emidio Vergani, and Sabino Chialà (Milan: Centro Ambrosiano, 2007), 129–57.

time of the writing of his sermon, the middle of the 480s.[21] The principal actor in this decade's divisive debates is never mentioned or even referred to in this *mēmrā*. While the parrot is Isaac's protagonist, it was Peter the Fuller, the patriarch of Antioch at various times (470–1, 475–6, 485–8), who brought about the theological controversy that widened an already dangerous rift among Christians in the city.[22] His innovation was short-lived, but significant within the Christological debates taking place at the time. From this distance, it was a minor alteration to ritual practice; the so-called Addition constituted the supplemental phrase "who was crucified for us" to the Trisagion.[23] Rafał Kosiński explains that the motivation behind the Addition was "…in all probability precisely to reinforce the Christological interpretation of the hymn by stressing that the Logos had truly incarnated and suffered."[24]

Little else is known about Peter, except through unfriendly chronicles written by his opponents, and no known writings of his survive. He was evidently interested in liturgical practice and was also a strong anti-Chalcedonian activist. Banished and exiled several times, Peter was opposed by imperial forces, yet apparently maintained much popular support throughout his years in and around power.

Isaac perceived that the Chalcedonian definition of Christ's nature—fully human and fully divine—came to imply that it was Jesus' human nature that was crucified and died on the Cross, not the divine. Isaac argued that the suffering of a human being was ineffective and insufficient

---

[21] See Andrea U. De Giorgi and A. Asa Eger, *Antioch: A History* (London: Routledge, 2021), *v. sub ind.*, and more broadly Lucy Parker, *Symeon Stylites the Younger and Late Antique Antioch: From Hagiography to History* (Oxford: Oxford University Press, 2022), 16–54.

[22] See Rafał Kosiński, "Peter the Fuller, Patriarch of Antioch (471–488)," *Byzantinoslavica* 68, no. 1 (2010): 49–73, and Daniel L. Schwartz, "Peter the Fuller—ܦܛܪܘܣ ܩܨܪܐ," in *The Syriac Biographical Dictionary*, ed. David A. Michelson [Syriaca.org: The Syriac Reference Portal, 2016, http://syriaca.org/person/2474], as well as John Meyendorff, *Imperial Unity and Christian Divisions: The Church 450–680 A.D.* (Crestwood, NY: St. Vladimir's Seminary Press, 1989), 107, 194–202, and 217 (the Addition is mentioned at 200, but not Isaac and his parrot), and Aloys Grillmeier and Theresia Hainthaler, *Christ in the Christian Tradition. Vol. 2. From the Council of Chalcedon (451) to Gregory the Great (590–604). Part 2. The Church of Constantinople in the Sixth Century*, trans. John Cawte and Pauline Allen (London: Mowbray, 1995), 252–62.

[23] On the Addition, see van Esbroeck, "The Memra on the Parrot by Isaac of Antioch", 465–9.

[24] Kosiński, "Peter the Fuller", 70.

for humanity's salvation. It was God (that is, Jesus) who had to suffer on the Cross to redeem humanity,

> When (Satan) schemed against the Cross of God through craftiness,
> so that one might confess the crucifixion of a human being, instead of God.
> When he schemed to insert the death and suffering of a human being,
> instead of the suffering and death which is of God who sets all free (ll. 125–8).

Isaac further rejects the conception of Christ being the indwelling of the Logos in a human nature as an instance of paganism,

> One whom they call a dwelling-place, and name him 'temple' and nature,
> for by two natures they schemed to erect two idols (ll.131–2).[25]

The Syriac author Aksenāyā (d. 523) was also supportive of the Addition and traveled the region to boost support for the initiative on behalf of Peter the Fuller. Once Peter regained the patriarchate, he appointed Aksenāyā ('the stranger') to the bishopric of Mabbug, and Aksenāyā took the name of Philoxenos, and became one of the foremost advocates of the Miaphysite interpretation as a theologian, controversialist, and bishop. Both men were completely won over to Peter the Fuller's Addition. However each arrived at that firm belief, they were theological allies on this contentious point.

ONE DAY IN ANTIOCH

There is no record of the circumstances that brought Isaac to Antioch from his home in Edessa, most likely during the third episcopate of Peter the Fuller (probably 484–5). While Isaac does refer to the terrible events and riots, arising from the use and prohibition of the Addition,[26] he does

---

[25] See Jaroslav Pelikan, *The Christian Tradition: A History of the Development of Doctrine. Vol. 1: The Emergence of the Catholic Tradition (100–600)* (Chicago: University of Chicago Press, 1971), 251–5.

[26] David S. Wallace-Hadrill, *Christian Antioch: A Study of Early Christian Thought in the East* (Cambridge: Cambridge University Press, 1982), esp. 6–10. Violence and unrest were recurrent from the mid-fourth century regarding taxation and Roman imperial control. The unrest during Isaac's period was engendered by the support of Emperors Leo I (r. 457–74) and Zeno (r. 474–91) of the decisions of Chalcedon in 451, which were opposed by the Miaphysite position of Peter the Fuller and Philoxenos of Mabbug.

not imply that he himself encountered any difficulty, let alone witnessed any altercations.

The modern separation between theological propositions and doctrines, and governmental laws and policies, did not exist at that time. Theological innovations were enforced or prohibited by both ecclesiastical and secular authorities, eliciting a wide range of responses and protests, which at times turned violent. What Isaac does describe and at great length is his witnessing of a parrot's recitations amid an irate gathering outside the ancient St. Peter's Church. The crowd was demanding the removal of the Addition, but a parrot's voice emerged clearly, emphatically, and persuasively. The parrot confronted and shamed them by crying "Holy, Holy."

That is as far as the narrative goes, for the rest of the *mēmrā* is focused on theological argument and exhortation targeted at the congregation to affirm the One True Nature of Christ. Given the frenetic passions at play among the populace during this period, the incident of a parrot reciting the Trisagion correctly is not implausible, and certainly memorable and highly teachable for Isaac.

Isaac the Miaphysite

Isaac of Antioch no longer needed to be persuaded about the orthodoxy of the Addition or the emerging Miaphysite refutation of Chalcedon. In the *mēmrā* directly preceding Isaac's parrot sermon in Bedjan's collection entitled "On the Passibility and Impassibility of God, the Word made Flesh,"[27] Isaac begins with the commonly accepted notion of knowledge and learning in Late Antiquity.

> Our faith is not a new thing; let us not make it new by retorts.
> Our learning is not that of a beginner; let us not bring to it an interpretation.
> We will not find it in a new way to seek to find God.
> As He was, He is; He does not change with time. [725: 1–4]

While the precise dates of his compositions are not known, Isaac wrote elsewhere at length about these theological issues, focusing on the primary dividing line between the Chalcedonian and Miaphysite confessions—the possibility of human knowledge about the human-divine

---

[27] Bedjan, *Homiliae S. Isaaci Syri Antiocheni*, Number 60: 725–37.

nature of Jesus Christ. Two examples of Isaac's examination of how one can and cannot know the nature of Christ follow.

The Miaphysite confession regarding the One United Nature of Christ insists that the human being cannot comprehend how Christ's united nature happens in real time. All one can do is to accept the reality, and not try to probe or investigate how and in what measure the pieces fit together. This position targeted the decisions of Chalcedon, and later the so-called 'nestorian' definitions of Christ in the Church of the East. Miaphysites charged that those opponents were attempting to define precisely in human language what Christ was made of.

In that same *mēmrā* noted above, directly preceding the Isaac's parrot sermon, "On the Passibility and Impassibility of God, the Word made Flesh," Isaac proclaims emphatically "the crucifixion of God." Two passages can stand here as exemplary of this position,

> Confess that he formed you from the dust; do not investigate how he exists. Bow down to him who saved you by his Only Begotten; do not investigate who is his Begetter.[28]

> They (the arrogant) do not bow on account of salvation, but in order to examine how it is.
> They do not confess about grace, but they debate whereby it exists.[29]

In a different genre of poetry, a *sūghītā* (a short poetic work intended for worship), "On the Blessed Virgin Mary and Those who Pry (or Investigate),"[30] Isaac depicts Mary delivering a soliloquy explaining the Miaphysite nature of her son, Jesus. Mary, after all, was there! 'Mary's' points of complaint (the term is attributed to her) were the issues of human knowability and investigation of the nature of God and Christ, with the corollary that Christ is One Nature.

> The teachers should not investigate the Son, your Saviour,
> for God is your Lord, **and** a human being with you. (12)
> He is God above, and he is human below;
> above as well as below, one child is not Two (13).

> Let him not be divided into two, he is one, let him not be split up;
> The Only-Begotten is the Son, and certainly, there is no other Son (28).

---

[28] Bedjan, *Homiliae S. Isaaci Syri Antiocheni*, Number 60: 726.7–8.
[29] Bedjan, *Homiliae S. Isaaci Syri Antiocheni*, Number 60: 726.21–2.
[30] Bickell, *S. Isaaci Antiocheni*, I: vii.78–84 (British Library Additional Ms 17141, ff. 100b).

Mary also countered docetic challenges that implied that Jesus only "seemed" or "appeared" (δοκέω—"I seem") to be really human, a ghost-like divinity. This was an early church tendency that Isaac recognized still had currency:

> He did not receive a body from the watchers, and descend to me,
> He was seen in my body, and God is with you (23).
> From me and in me he was armed, and he went out against death,
> and although he put on the body, One is the Son, not Two (24).

Isaac of Antioch deploys a remarkable incident to argue for the Miaphysite confession of christology, which was gaining strength in the latter part of the fifth century. In several metrical homilies, Isaac emphasizes that Christ is One United Person and Nature, fully human and fully divine, accomplished by a method beyond human comprehension that should not be investigated. His opposition to dyophysite or two-nature christologies is that these positions create multiple personalities of Christ, and generally make Jesus' human nature the sole location of his death and suffering. For Isaac, Christ is One, and it is Christ God suffering and dying on the Cross that provides the incomparable power of the resurrection. God saves us, not a human being.

Trajectory of the Mēmrā

The diversity and complexity of the elements and pieces in this long *mēmrā* on the parrot raise the issues of purpose, occasion, and audience. Whether this is a composite homily, gathered from several sources and occasions, is an open question that is difficult to assess. By the fact that all the extant manuscripts show the same obvious lacuna, we know that there was an older Ur-Text, probably containing the missing narrative, but perhaps not including different sections at different stages. The Cloud of Witnesses section is a candidate for later insertion as a stand-alone piece. Its length—291 lines or 27% of the total homily—creates a temporary divergence from the principal themes of the *mēmrā*.

The *mēmrā* functions as a pastoral and theological exhortation and instruction in support of the Addition to the Trisagion, which lays the critical theological foundation for the Miaphysite/anti-Chalcedonian understanding of Christ and the Gospel. Along with Philoxenos,[31] Isaac sees the event of the Suffering Crucified God as a fundamentally soteriological initiative of God towards humanity. To remove God from the Cross is to negate any possibility of salvation for God's people.

The occasion for this *mēmrā* is a liturgical (or perhaps educational) setting in which Isaac presents 'acts' of varying pace and content that maintain the attention of the congregation and periodically ignite their enthusiasm. Isaac accelerates the tempo to engage the people emotionally and spiritually in order to affirm and participate in the joy of God the Word's salvific role on the Cross. He alternates by slowing down so that the congregation may absorb new information, resting before the next movement begins. When and where such a liturgical (or, again, educational) setting might have taken place is not known, since the *mēmrā* does not focus upon commemorating a saint or any kind of occasion, but upon a theological argument.

Outline of Mēmrā on the Bird Who Sang the Trisagion

- a. Proemion to the Cross (ll. 1–74)
- b. When the Parrot Squawked (ll. 75–148)
- c. Isaac Completes the Parrot's Song (ll. 149–226)
- d. Isaac's Praise for the Parrot and the Cross (ll. 227–344)
- e. The Nature of the Parrot as the Divine Sign (*Rēmzā*) (ll. 345–450)
- f. Rebuke of Deniers of the Addition to the Trisagion (ll. 451–594)
- g. Pastoral Encouragement Not to Lose Faith (ll. 595–636)
- h. A Cloud of Witnesses (ll. 637–928)
- i. Understanding What the Parrot Sang (ll. 929–1008)
- j. Last Word, Same as the First: The Felicity of the Cross (ll. 1009–68)

(a) *Proemion to the Cross (ll. 1–74)*

The first section is an Invocation/Proemion addressed to the Cross (ll. 1–74), which demonstrates the priority of the salvific function of the

---

[31] See *Three Letters of Philoxenus of Mabbug, Bishop of Mabbogh (485–519): Being the Letter to the Monks, the First Letter to the Monks of Beth-Gaugal, and the Letter to the Emperor Zeno*, ed. and trans. Arthur Adolphe Vaschalde (Rome: Tipografia della Reale Accademia dei Lincei, 1902), especially "The Letter to the Monks," 93–105 (English), 127–45 (Syriac).

Cross. The Resurrection is not ignored, but the Cross is the locus of salvation. At the very beginning is marked Isaac's understanding of the Cross' role, as well as the Parrot's, "Your Cross is a speaking pen, for through it the silent speak" (l. 9).[32] A lengthy list of adjectives for the Cross are recited in ll. 27–71: lyre and harp, pleasant voice, vessel, burning fire, pleasant spring, beautiful bridge, hot oven, strong wall, tree of life, mighty tower, stairway, swift wing, gate of truth, key of life. These metaphors transform the gruesomeness of the Cross into a medium of transition to new life, establishing for the congregation an enlightened perspective on the central symbol of Christianity.

(b) *When the Parrot Squawked (ll. 75–148)*

The second section then goes directly to the day in Antioch when Isaac encountered the Parrot. The first change of pace presents a dramatic narrative that is arresting, yet conveys the striking manner by which the Parrot awakened Isaac to the centrality of the Addition to worship and to orthodox faith. Isaac defines the meaning of the Addition in opposition to the Satanic schemes to make a new god—the Chalcedonian and Nestorian two-natured Christ, a four-person Trinity or quaternity (ܪܒܝܥܝܘܬܐ)—and therefore alerts the congregation to the reality of a pagan polytheism surreptitiously imposed upon their worship.[33] The concept of a quaternity is the construct of the Miaphysites against both the Chalcedonian confession and the Church of the East. The latter two confessions, it should be noted, did not perceive or accept that they were altering the Trinity.

(c) *Isaac Completes the Parrot's Song (ll. 149–226)*

The third section is Isaac's joyful response to the epiphany of the bird and his explanation of the Addition's theological implications. Isaac accomplishes this goal first by reciting a long chain, beginning with the "Holy, Holy God" refrain of the Trisagion (149–226), that utilizes the

---

[32] References are to Bedjan's edition (737:17)—ܘܒܐܝܕܗ ܗܘ ܡܡܠܠ ܗܘ ܐܠܡܐ܂ ܟܬܒܐ.

[33] Philoxenos of Mabbug labels this 'quaternity' as paganism as well. *Letter of Mar Aksenaya to the Monks*, "For he who counts another man with God, introduces a quaternity in his doctrine and destroys the dogma of the Holy Trinity" (100).
ܗܘ ܝܢ ܗܢܐ ܒܪܢܫܐ ܐܚܪܢܐ ܡܢ ܕܥܡ ܐܠܗܐ. ܡܥܠ ܪܒܝܥܝܘܬܐ ܒܬܘܕܝܬܗ (142)

heightened awareness of the congregation into a 'call and response' sequence. This is the central theological segment of the *mēmrā*.

An Unheard-of Epiphany

Isaac is struck by the serendipity of the moment, a revelatory event that awakened Isaac as to why the Addition to the Trisagion is the correct and necessary interpretation of the Gospel. The Parrot's squawking of the Addition, "who was crucified for us," had taken on the form of a slogan, and now Isaac fills in the implications of this Addition, and consequently explains the Miaphysite perception of the nature of Christ.

Isaac arrives at St. Peter's to encounter a crowd gathered around something unheard of, but now being heard—"a wise bird who was chirping the faith" (l. 82). The people were drawn to listen to the bird out of curiosity, but once Isaac had taken it all in, he declared to himself, "this is a Sign of God, which has been stirred up through his providence " (l. 90). This was the Kairos moment, for in the wake of "the horrors that had happened" (l. 97), referring to the violent riots of past years, the sound of a parrot squawked through the shouting and general din.

Satan's Schemes and Nebuchadnezzar

The controversy at this stage still primarily centered around the Addition to the Trisagion, and not yet the anti-Chalcedonian debates that would rage towards the end of the fifth century and into the sixth. Isaac sees the schismatics or Chalcedonians imposing, as it were, an intellectual image or idol which he compares to Nebuchadnezzar's idol in Daniel 2—introducing paganism into the Church. "As two natures and sons, it attempted to erect a division and make a quaternity in the mystery of the Trinity" (ll. 103–04). Isaac perceives the operational dynamic of the Chalcedonian party as "Satan's schemes" that had the ultimate purpose of removing the salvific trajectory of the Orthodox.

Holy, Holy God ...

A dramatic section, a call and response between preacher and congregation, is begun as Isaac mimics the parrot's crying out three times "Holy, Holy (God)," amplifying for the congregation and reader the theological detail which the parrot's voice evokes in their minds and souls. Isaac begins with the Addition, but inevitably moves to a pithy exposition of Miaphysite Christology, quite similar in vocabulary and tone to that of Philoxenos of Mabbug who advocated strongly for the Addition during this same period.

One cannot pray the Trisagion without Christ, and Isaac's initial charge is that the schismatics have defiled the Cross by substituting a human being (the human nature of Christ) in place of the Suffering of God the Word, removing or negating the soteriological benefit of God's travail on the Cross (ll. 123–40, 171–82). To Isaac's mind, the Chalcedonian theology denies and rejects a number of characteristics of Christ: his birth and infancy, and that he was born as a temple and dwelt in it as a human being (ll. 183–90). Isaac rejects the claim of others that a human fetus was joined to the Word (ll. 191–2). God the Word had defeated the passions by his Cross, yet there were some who dared to say that the divine nature had fled the Cross to avoid suffering, substituting the human nature on the Cross to suffer (ll. 97–8).

The latter stanzas of the "Holy, Holy" refrain (ll. 201–26) focus unabashedly on the Miaphysite positions that countered Chalcedon, although he turns aside in one stanza (ll. 211–2) to denounce "the wicked Nestorians," who have slandered God the Word to whom the Virgin gave birth, by saying that he was a human being.

Philoxenos and others consistently lumped Chalcedon with the so-called Nestorians since both were dyophysites, that is, that Christ had two natures, human and divine. The Nestorian heresy was generally employed by the Miaphysites as an intellectual construct, a straw man, easy to oppose and refute. But during this period, the Church of the East, situated primarily in the rival Sasanian Empire, was little known to the West Syrian Church and was still developing its distinctive Christological understanding.

Isaac's declarations are straightforward. The first is the basic definition, "Holy, Holy God, who is One in his Person; some divide the natures: one is human and one is God" (ll. 201–2). The Philoxenian emphasis follows on 'becoming'– "Who became a human being through his love, that is to say, he is God, while at the same time he is also a human being" (ll. 203–4), and defined emphatically by "who is holy in his essence, but in the likeness of one of the saints, some wicked ones supposed him [to be]" (ll. 209–10). This latter couplet demonstrates again a principal concern of Isaac, in which some interpreters reduce Christ's divine characteristics to that of a holy person, that is, an extraordinary human being, but not fully divine.

(d) *Isaac's Praise for the Parrot and the Cross (ll. 227–344)*

Isaac changes the rhythm again by offering his own spiritual insights on what the Addition means to him. It is not clear whether Isaac had been undecided up to this juncture, but this homily and others on comparable themes serve to affirm his conviction. Another lengthy chain ensues (ll. 265–342), beginning with "I praised him" (ܫܒܚܬܗ).

> I praised him concerning his humility, for by it our humility was exalted, and concerning his wealthy renunciation, for by it our poverty becomes rich (ll. 273–4).

> I praised him because he is without time and without beginning, and because he became embodied, they wrote about him in years and in days (ll. 299–300).

> I praised him on account of his eating; he was not lacking what he desired, yet was hungry,
> for by it he gave his holy body to eat to the hungry whom Satan had afflicted (ll. 309–10).

> I praised him because of his resurrection, for through it our mortality was resurrected; Death and Satan died by it, for they had killed our humanity (ll. 325–6).

(e) *The Nature of the Parrot as the Divine Sign (Rēmzā) (ll. 345–450)*

The fifth section slows down and returns to the icon of the parrot to consider the nature of a bird as a vehicle for proclamation. Isaac reminds his audience that it was the parrot that awakened his thinking.

> My mind pushed me all the more, for it shouted my words in truth;
> by hearing the voice of the bird, who spoke words of truth (ll. 357–8).

> I meditated even more so that it proclaimed about life without death,
> for the death of the Crucified endures, which the bird also proclaimed (ll. 363–4).

In attempting to figure out why it was a bird that pushed him to think faithfully, Isaac utilizes the Syriac concept of the Sign (*rēmzā* ܪܡܙܐ), a divine force that influences actions and decisions, although the Sign is never explicitly mentioned in Scripture. Isaac is reserved in this identification, but understands the Parrot as a divine agent whose purpose is not to bring about change by speaking openly and provocatively.

> Its voice was sent for reproof, her voice which its harp proclaimed,
> whether it is from learning, or from the Sign of God.
> If it is his own learning, that is to say, it means it gave it to you so that you may learn;
> and if it is a gift from His Sign, see, the power of His mercy is revealed (ll. 387–90).

But what kind of agent is this? The Parrot says the truth that has never before been said.

> But a bird such as this? A bird has never spoken,
> yet I have not heard (anything like) this, not even from a person have I received it
> (ll. 427–8).

This is a new voice, which was heard uttered by a bird (l. 431).

(f) *Rebuke of Deniers of the Addition to the Trisagion (ll. 451–594)*

Having established that the Parrot is the 'personification' of the Sign or Signal of God, Isaac intensifies the dramatic narration by turning to rebuke and curse those who deny the truth of the Addition to the Trisagion. They are shamed by the voice of the parrot who proclaims the crucifixion of God (ll. 451–7), and by more than the voice. In an image famously used by Ephrem, "Let them be ashamed by the stretching out of her wings, which depict the mysteries of the cross" (l. 461), the living icon of the bird.

> Let the deniers who malign the truth be embarrassed by the bird,
> for in hidden and public matters, the glory of the Crucified one is inscribed on it.
> When it spread out its wings, it depicted the beautiful image of the Cross,
> and when it opened its mouth, it chirped its faith and its truth (ll. 463–6).

Isaac begins a meditation (ll. 463–507) regarding the phenomenon of the parrot's revelation. While Isaac recognizes that a bird neither speaks nor theologizes in a human fashion, in this instance the nature of the parrot was formed by God so that she might become a vehicle of revelation, in many ways superior to what human beings are able to convey. "It maintains a single confession in the mind that its Creator gave to her" (l. 477).

(g) *Pastoral Encouragement Not to Lose Faith (ll. 595–636)*

In the confrontational environment of Antioch regarding the Trisagion, Isaac again shifts the tone and spends a significant section (ll. 531–90) exhorting the faithful not to give in to doubt about their beliefs. First, by not associating with those who nurture doubts about the nature of the crucified one and so are susceptible to error. "Do not exchange the truth for gold, nor sell your faith, lest you inherit the noose of Iscariot the murderer" (ll. 587–8).

Isaac closes this part of the *mēmrā* with positive injunctions to individuals to keep up the good fight and not resort to heresy and evil. "Put on the [shoes of] readiness of the Gospel, and trample the goads of the left, and bring low Satan and his ranks by the name of the Crucified one" (ll. 615–6). "You are eating the sacrifice of his body; you owe the sacrifice of your body" (l. 621).

(h) *A Cloud of Witnesses (ll. 637–928)*

The longest section of the *mēmrā* is entitled by van Esbroeck "The Faith of the Fathers as a Model."[34] Following the template of Hebrews 11 and other works, Isaac marches through a lengthy number of Old Testament and Apocryphal personalities who "by faith" did remarkable things, according to the clarion call in Hebrews 11. *The Book of Steps* devotes *Mēmrā* Nine to a similar prose recital of the great figures and prophets of the Old Testament who followed God's will, even though they were often required to perform violent tasks and were granted entrance into the Kingdom of Heaven only after the Apostles entered.[35] In

---

[34] van Esbroeck, "The Memra on the Parrot by Isaac of Antioch", 470, who also stresses the importance of the Epistle to the Hebrews for Isaac's composition (470–1).
[35] Michael Kmosko, *Liber Graduum*, Patrologia Syriaca, vol. 3 (Paris: Firmon-Didot et Socii, 1926), Mēmrā 9: cols. 189–248; (English translation) Robert A. Kitchen and M.F.G. Parmentier, *The Book of Steps: The Syriac Liber Graduum*, Cistercian Studies, vol. 196 (Kalamazoo, MI: Cistercian Publications, 2004), 83–107.

Mēmrā 97, "On the Praises of John the Baptist," Jacob of Serugh gives two similar lists of Old Testament heroes.[36]

It is evident that Isaac's structure of his 'cloud of witnesses' borrowed elements from previous works, in particular the renowned section, "Now let us praise famous men," in the *Wisdom of Ben Sirach*, chapters 44–50. Sirach's inclusion of several post-exilic figures—Zerubbabel, Joshua ben Jehozadak, Nehemiah, and Simon ben Onias—is distinctive from other such saints' lists. Isaac's list is the longest found so far in Syriac literature and includes Zerubbabel, Joshua ben Jehozadak, Tobit, a number of other personalities from the Apocrypha, and then adds Judas and the other Maccabean brothers who are not mentioned in Sirach.

Thomas Long senses in Hebrews 11 a form of the rhythmic call and response found especially in African American congregations, but certainly not absent in earlier charismatic congregations.[37] It is the opening refrain, "by faith," which Hebrews 11 employs, that Isaac adopts to build the crescendo as the saints go marching in.

Isaac does wax eloquently upon reaching the end of his 'cloud,' being inspired by the journey of these faithful ones and joining them along the narrow road filled with afflictions and suffering (ll. 929–1008), a section which tries to demonstrate the purpose of the 'cloud of witnesses' within the total *mēmrā*. One line appears to indicate the intention to connect the Trisagion episodes with those who journeyed by faith: "All these illustrious ones, and there are many more than these, sensed the mysteries of the crucified one, and became rich in the Trinity" (ll. 937–8).

(i) *Understanding What the Parrot Sang (ll. 929–1008)*

In the penultimate section of the *mēmrā* after the long 'Cloud,' Isaac once more slows down the pace, spelling out the deeper meaning of the parrot's chirping for those faithful who have heard her. The parrot spoke of participation in salvation, which as a non-human they would not be able to experience.

---

[36] Paul Bedjan, *Homiliae Selectae Mar-Jacobi Sarugensis* (Leipzig: Harrassowitz, 1907), III: 97.687–710.

[37] Thomas G. Long, *Hebrews* (Louisville: Westminster John Knox Press, 1997), 112–29. Long notes that in African-American congregations there is a motto on how to preach a good sermon, "Start low, go slow, reach higher, strike fire, sit down in a storm" (112).

> That [bird] spoke about his salvation, although it did not taste of his body.
> You, give thanks for his redemption, for you are eating his body and his blood.
> That [bird] sang of his holiness, although it did not experience his forgiveness.
> You, give thanks for his forgiveness, for by his holiness you have been absolved.
> That [bird] offered praise for his death, although resurrection was not promised to it.
> You, proclaim his suffering and his death, for you are reveling in his life.
> That [bird] who did not inherit his promises, was diligent to sing his praises;
> As for you, everything he had, he gave to you, shout and proclaim his honours
> (ll. 1013–20).

Human beings also receive from the crucified one's suffering, death, and shame something that one is not able to do on his own,

> Something which the ear did not hear, the sufferings of the crucified one gave to you.
> Fill the ear with your words, the words of faith.
> Something which the eye did not see, the death of the Crucified one gave to you.
> Become a vision to the one seeing, and praise him before the judges.
> Something that did not come to mind, the shame of the Crucified one gave to you;
> May your heart become a spring of life, and praise and proclaim his thanksgiving.
> (ll. 1021–6).

Analogously, therefore, the faithful human is not able to sense the grace of God and Christ except through the revelation of the crucified one, and the parrot cannot experience or comprehend the glory of the resurrection. The analogy is somewhat strained, but the emphasis is upon the inability of creatures intellectually to grasp the mystery of God who nevertheless effects our (human) salvation. The parrot possesses speech, and the human as another of God's creatures has the same relationship to God and Christ as the parrot—a radical conclusion.

(j) *Last Word, Same as the First: The Felicity of the Cross (ll. 1009–68)*

Isaac concludes the *mēmrā* as he began, praising the virtue and benefit of Cross-centered theology, and urging his congregation and readers to do the same.

> In the crucified one I have found these virtues without number;
> preach his faith, for even the bird declared it (ll. 1009–10).

In the initial section of the homily, Isaac depicted the salvific reality of the Cross and the Crucified with a series of positive metaphors. In this final section, he exhorts his readers to embody them in their lives. "In the Crucified one find life, and tread upon the neck of death; he is for you a bridge, so cross over to the light of the Trinity" (ll. 1037–8), which plays off the earlier confession, "Your Cross is a beautiful bridge, which crosses over to the abode of life; by which I will cross over to your knowledge, and will praise your crucifixion" (ll. 55–6).

Isaac urges the reader to become a temple trumpet (ll. 1043–4), a true laborer (ll. 1045–6), and a living trumpet (ll. 1047–8) so that one may preach and proclaim the Gospel of New Life acquired for him by the Crucified One.

Isaac's *mēmrā* appears to be a loose collection of literary pieces, but it is a carefully artisaned and balanced work to describe and demonstrate, exhort and challenge, as well as to rebuke, so that the congregation may be inspired and energized to follow the God who was crucified for us. With the agency of the parrot as the Sign of God (*Rēmzā*), language is the medium, even that of non-humans.

A fitting stanza to conclude is one that may be read as a play-on-words worthy of the entire *mēmrā*, "He became for you a ladder, so that you might reach the higher life; the Father and the Son testify to me, and the Spirit that chirped through the Apostles" (ll. 1041–2).

CHAPTER 2

Translation: Isaac of Antioch's Mēmrā on the Parrot

Abstract This chapter provides a full translation of the surviving text written by Isaac of Antioch in reaction to his encounter in the 480s with a parrot who revealed to him the correct position to take in relation to a theological controversy roiling the city—an addition to the Trisagion prayer introduced by the divisive patriarch Peter the Fuller. Little historical information survives concerning this controversy, and Isaac's indirect account of the events is unique testimony to the complexity and significance of the dispute. The text also reveals important considerations of animal revelation and of the relations between animals and divinity, considerations that distinguish Isaac as a noteworthy author not only for his witness to contemporary events, but also for his ruminations on animality and God.

Keywords Isaac of Antioch • Addition controversy • Peter the Fuller • Syriac Christianity • Parrots • Cloud of witnesses

Isaac of Antioch's Bird Who Sang the Trisagion
Paul Bedjan, Homiliae S. Isaaci Syri Antiocheni *(Paris, 1903)*
737:5–788:15

© The Author(s), under exclusive license to Springer Nature Switzerland AG 2024
R. A. Kitchen, G. Peers, The Bird Who Sang the Trisagion *of Isaac of Antioch*, Palgrave Studies in Animals and Literature,
https://doi.org/10.1007/978-3-031-60077-7_2

[737:5] *Mēmrā* 61, which is composed by Mar Isaac of Antioch, concerning that Parrot which cried out, "Hagios O Theos" in the city of Antioch.

1. Invocation addressed to the Cross

Give birth in me, my Lord, by your mercy,	a *mēmrā* full of benefits;
I shall speak concerning the Parrot	who chirped to us the faith.
Awaken my silent mind	by the living word of your knowledge;
I shall recount a great wonder	that your Sign[1] stirs up in the natures.
5 Become for me a teacher and I shall discern	in the great book of your wisdom,
in which treasures are hidden,	incomprehensible secrets.
My tongue was made a skilled scribe,	a learned pen for your ideas;
inscribe with it according to your knowledge	the sublime riches of your Cross.
Your Cross is a speaking pen,	for through it the silent have spoken;
10 [738] let its living voice speak through me	its hymns through the pen of my tongue.
The construction of your Cross, my Lord,	has stirred up gentle sounds in the world,
for at their sound error trembled,	and the demons, its servants, howled.
For it became like a harp	bearing sweet hymns,
and rendered the disturbed world peaceful	from the conflict of the idols.
15 By the sound which it emitted from its wings,	it calmed the regions of the world
from thieves who belched forth error	by idols and false gods.
By the word which it proclaimed from your womb,	it stirred up the womb of Sheol,[2]
and rendered peaceful the womb of the earth	by its unchanging truth.
Your living person spoke through it	a saving and reverent word;
20 and the mute natures replied to it	praise and glory and honour.
Through its sweetness the earth became pleasant,	and its bitterness was sweetened,
and he drew his sweet voice	to come to its pleasant taste.
By the sweet springs of his hymns,	he cleansed the bitterness of the dragon,
and the pure body of his truth	blossomed like a flash of light.
25 By the sound of the lyre of your Cross,	he cast down the lyre of idols;
and by the song of your praise,	the great mockery of those who opposed you.

---

[1] *Rēmză*, technical term for the divine movement in nature.
[2] The place of the dead, into which Christ entered after death on the Cross and killed Death and liberated Adam and Eve, and all the other dead souls (Mt 27:52–53).

Your Cross is a sweet lyre, whose voice strengthens the weak,
and they bring down and defeat the warriors and the tyrants in the struggle.

Your Cross is a sweet harp, that captures minds with it,
30 for they have fixed their bodies on the Cross, since they cannot repel its sweetness.

[739] Your Cross is a pleasant voice that has enraptured souls after it,
and fire and sword and iron combs did not cut them off from its love.

Your Cross is a living harp whose sound has made the demons flee,
and caused souls to hasten after it on the road crowded with afflictions.

35 Your Cross is a harp of remedies, which has healed a sick world,
and by the sweetness of its songs, it has mitigated all of its illnesses.

Your salvific finger touched it, the living and spiritual voice,
and proclaimed the Word of God and drove away the gods from the earth.

Your Cross is an instrument by which your salvific voice spoke, giving life to all,
40 and summoned the entire world to come to enjoy its banquet.

Your Cross is a lyre of wisdom, which was spoken against despicableness,
and defeated the wisdom of the wise by the simple words that they spoke through it.

Your Cross is a harp of the Spirit, which healed the world from error,
like the harp of the son of Jesse that drove out the [evil] spirit from Saul.[3]

45 Your salvific word sang through it, and the spirit of his torment fled
to the world, which loved illness, which the evil one had given birth through idols.

The salvific finger of your person played new melodies upon it,
and through its speaking strings made the evil spirits flee.

Your Cross is a burning fire which tests and refines the mind,
50 and judges the thoughts of the heart and the inner movements of the emotions.

[740] The senses are stirred up by it, secretly and openly,
for it allows perception so that in wonder all may sense it.

Your Cross is a pleasant spring, which makes eloquent waters flow;
it gave me drink from them and I will speak about its word in every dialect.

55 Your Cross is a beautiful bridge, which crosses over to the abode of life;
by which I will convert to your knowledge, and praise your crucifixion.

Your Cross is a hot kiln, which purifies thoughts;
by its rays [of light] it purifies my mind, so that I may speak about your Lordship.

Your Cross is the tree of life, whose fruit resurrects the dead;
60 by which my thoughts will be revived, and I shall speak about its life.

Your Cross is a sturdy wall, which rebels do not subdue;
it assured me by its peace, and I shall speak about the tranquility of your crucifixion.

Your Cross is a mighty tower by which a person ascends to heaven;
let my mind ascend on it to you, and because of your humility I praise you.

---

[3] 1 Sam 16: 14–23.

65 Your Cross is a stairway, which ascends from the depths to the heights;
on it I will ascend to your parent, and I shall praise you because of your salvation.

Your Cross is a light wing, which makes heavy things fly;
let my mind fly and soar on it, and speak concerning your glory.

Your Cross is the true gate, which invites everything to grace;
70 through it I enter and by your grace I shall praise you for your grace.

Your Cross is the key of life, which opens muzzled mouths,
[741] for the muzzled also are eloquent, with wonder they shall offer its glory.

The Cross, which does new things, summoned me to wonder at its work;
listeners, let your minds come here, and be pleased by new things.

2. When the Bird Sang in Antioch

75 On the occasion you had summoned me to enter   the chief of cities, the city of Antioch,
a singular marvel encountered me, and I greatly wondered at its sight.

Before I saw it, I heard its voice, and my mind urged me to see it;
and the marvel is timeless,[4] for it came to rebuke [Antioch's] evilness.

As I was thinking, going to the meeting place of the apostolate,
80 to that church that Simeon had built, the chosen apostle of God.

As I was astonished by that same voice, the sight suddenly came upon me
of that wise bird, who was chirping the faith.

I saw the crowd of people that had gathered and heard the new thing that had happened;
I also joined the crowd, so that I might reap its benefits.

85 While everyone heard the bird according to his discernment,
I collected my mind carefully to discern what it means.[5]

Realizing what time it is, and by what the voice is;
I was amazed at the occasion and the voice grappling with one another in the contest.

I discerned and was greatly amazed, and thought to myself,
90 "this is the Sign[6] of God that has been stirred up through his providence."

[742] The novice voice was not ordinary,
that a bird would cry out in the market   the faith of the Crucified one.

---

[4] Lit. 'against time'.
[5] Lit. 'a skilled assembly of meanings'.
[6] *Rēmzā*.

This is not a common sign, by which audacious things could be hidden,
for they had dared to doubt the truth of the crucifixion.
95 For at this time, see, they are taking up sides against one another;
the orthodox and the schismatics,[7] and a battle is pitted between them.
For after the atrocities that had happened on account of this in the city;[8]
There was this sight, and the sound of this bird.
While the conflict was still poised like a sword against the factions,
100 and error was urged upon its children, truth made its own prosper.
As the image was placed in the middle, which was not from [divine] essence;
a human being whom fraud had formed and its servant created a god.
As two natures and sons, it attempted to erect a division,
and make a quaternity[9] in the mystery of the Trinity.
105 While Satan was finagling to set up falsehood against truth,
and to impose paganism by another guise into the holy church.
As deceit through craftiness, he wished to devastate faith,
and by narrowness to introduce two objects of worship against the truth.
As the basilisk is coiled to disturb a clear spring,
110 [743] the church, in which the living water of truth is flowing.
As the seditious Satan by his custom, stood up as the most skilled,
and thrust a sword through the sides to slay the church by his jealousy.
When the ruler of iniquity stood up to bathe the church in blood,
to flourish his sword from the sides, and its blade licks up the blood.
115 When the sword of controversy is poised, and is thirsty for the blood of the saints,
the ministry of Satan is accomplished through wicked and insolent ones.
When the blade is unsheathed by him to devour the flesh of the true,
and tear down the bodies that have been nourished by the body and blood of God.
When the bow of iniquity is drawn and is armed[10] with an arrow of deceit,
120 the hand of deceit is steady to strike the heart of the true.
When the persecutor openly acts in another disguise,
so that through a mask of truth he may impose iniquity in the midst.

---

[7] Here the Miaphysites are the 'orthodox' and the Chalcedonians are the 'schismatics.'

[8] Riots between the two factions: those supporting Council of Chalcedon and those opposing (Miaphysites).

[9] The charge directed against dyophysite Christologies (Chalcedonian and 'Nestorian') that if Christ has two natures, human and divine, then there are two Sons and therefore four persons in the Trinity: Father, Spirit, Human Son, Divine Son.

[10] Lit. 'is full/filled'.

When Satan schemes
he introduces one confession for [another] confession
to defile the truth of the Cross,
to be imposed into the truth.

125 When he schemed against the Cross of God through craftiness,
so that one might confess the crucifixion
of a human being,
instead of God.

When he schemed to impose
instead of the suffering and death which is
the death and suffering of a human being,
of God, for by him he sets all free.

When Satan schemed
130 one that signs sprung forth
to make a new god,
and attached to the Only Begotten Son.

One whom they call a dweller,
[744] for by two natures they schemed
and name him temple and nature,
to erect two idols.

He is seeking to establish these things,
and to exchange one passion for another,
and to tear asunder the truth deceitfully,
salvation for no salvation.

135 He is seeking to establish our hope in a human being instead of God,
and to believe in the crucifixion of a human being, instead of that honourable one.

When Satan was troubled
and showed urgency
to introduce these things into the church,
through those people who do his will.

This hidden idol
140 just like that [idol] of Nebuchadnezzar,
was depicted and erected in the center,
which was depicted by graven images.[11]

As he established a new god,

and deceitfully, such as with gold,
and it was clothed with the garment of a human being,
the evil artisans fashioned it.

Deception was troubled,
and the appearance of the idol shone
just like Babylon, on account of the image,
with wickedness and falsehood.

145 When he roared Commandment,
and the other leaders with him,
which urged a single leader,
so that this image might be honoured.

He uses a threat
and death was threatened
against one who does not honour him,
against whoever dares and dishonours.

3. *Isaac Sings the Parrot's Song*

And just as Satan placed
150 this bird chirped,
this hidden idol in the middle,
since there still was a controversy.

I was standing and I heard its voice
[745] in order to rebuke the false idols
as it sang three times,
as three for the image of Babylon.

---

[11] Daniel 3: 1–30.

I heard the twittering of its mouth, 'Holy, Holy,' it said	that is like the word of a human being. to the Crucified one who saved all.[12]
155 I was amazed at the sound of its lyre, and as with the words in lullabies	which sang three times, it spoke the faith.
Holy, Holy God, that praise in which the crowded ranks	the voice of its chants proclaimed of seraphim were rejoicing.
Holy, Holy God, 160 that (crying) 'holy' by which	it sang three times, the company of heavenly watchers was renewed.
'Holy, Holy,' the voice that glory that is in the kingdom,	of its sweet lyre proclaimed by which the angels are nourished.
Holy, Holy God, that (crying) 'Holy' by which is sanctified	the voice of its harp resounded the bosom of the glorious church.
165 Holy, Holy God, in order to rebuke those who denied	the lyre of its voices sang the truth of the glory of God.
Holy, Holy God, against the impure who did not (cry) holy	its beautiful voice shouted out to God as was fitting.
Holy, Holy God, 170 "He bore this iniquity	the voice of the bird preached: and did not blot out creation."[13]
Holy, Holy God, and they confess the Cross of a human being	His Cross is defiled by a human, instead of that same honourable one.
Holy, Holy God,	instead of Him, his suffering is through that of another,
[746] and to the glory of his crucifixion,	they gave a human nature.
175 Holy, Holy God,	whose (crying) Holy is defiled by a human being,
and the voice of the deniers endures,	for they blaspheme his crucifixion.
Holy, Holy God, and they took and gave it to another,	for some people defiled his grace, so that he was not able to save all.
Holy, Holy God, 180 and confessed another who became great,	some defiled his humility, and lived by the grace of God.
Holy, Holy God, and took it to give to another	some defiled his salvation, who was empty of salvation.
Holy, Holy God, and by a human being they confess that he became	some defiled his renunciation, God by perfection.

---

[12] Trisagion Prayer: "Holy God, Holy [and] Mighty, Holy [and] Immortal, have mercy on us." The "twice Holy" is used simply as shorthand, because the *mēmrā* is a metrical poem of 7 + 7 syllables in each line. 'Qadish-Qadish-Qadish' are six syllables, so there is not enough syllable space for the whole refrain.

[13] Is 53: 4.

185 Holy, Holy God,
and joined with him a human being

some defiled his lordship,
who shall be worshipped like him.

Holy, Holy God,
the deniers defiled his being,
the insolent blasphemed and spoke impiously that he dwelt in a human being.

Holy, Holy God,
190 and said that he was born a temple,

some defiled his birth,
and dwelt in it as in a human being.

Holy, Holy God,
and said that a fetus was joined to him,

some defiled his infancy,
so that through it his will might be served.

Holy, Holy God,
and some iniquitous ones gave him

his birth and His Cross were defiled,
to another who was alien to him.

195 Holy, Holy God,
[**747**] yet they went to give his grace

who endured the sufferings of humanity,
to one whose suffering is in his nature.

Holy, Holy God,
who defeated the passions by His Cross,
yet the insolent reproached him that he had fled, so that suffering would not touch him.

Holy, Holy God,
200 and took and gave it to another

some denied his victory,
who was condemned through his nature.

Holy, Holy God,
but some divide the natures:

who is One in his Person;
one is human and one is God.[14]

Holy, Holy God,
that is to say, he is God,

who became a human being through his love,
while at the same time he is also a human being.

205 Holy, Holy God,
but some deniers accused falsely

for God is the Son of God,
that the Son of the Creator is a creature.

Holy, Holy God,
and that which is made means that it is

for the Maker is the Son of the Maker,
the People who made evil things.

Holy, Holy God,
210 but in the likeness of one of the saints,

who is holy in his essence,
some wicked ones supposed him [to be].

Holy, Holy God,
but the wicked Nestorians

whom the virgin gave birth in wonder,
slandered him that he was a human being.

Holy, Holy God,
and since he was worthy of glory,

who is the Lord of Glory,
they wrote wicked tracts.

215 Holy, Holy God,
and became richer than the creatures,

who opened his treasures on His cross,
yet the deniers defiled his virtues.

---

[14] Isaac's argument now shifts to the affirmation of the One United Nature of Christ, i.e., Miaphysite.

[748] Holy, Holy God, / yet the fools who mistook his humility / who performed mighty deeds by his humility, / said that he was weak.

Holy, Holy God, / 220 and by the passion of his crucifixion, / who was believed through his exploits, / he showed on earth his victories.

Holy, Holy God, / and revealed himself to sight, / who was hidden on high, / yet the despicable defamed his beauty.

Holy, Holy God, / yet some defiled ones assailed him / through whom humanity became sanctified, / in order to treat his dignity shamefully.

225 Holy, Holy God, / and during this special time, / who bore the reproach of humanity, / some defiled his truth.

4. *Praise for the Parrot and the Crucified One*

The voice of that wise bird / and by that (crying) 'holy' three times, / signaled to such as these, / it honored the faith.

For its lyre signified wisely / 230 I stood up and was filled with wonder / to such as these; / by the power that stirs its chants.

My mind became full of its meaning / and with wonder I departed from it, / which its delightful song gave to me, / after I was pleased by its sound.

My mind was sated by its banquet, / and with wonder I left it and went / and I was fed by its words, / to the table of its songs.

235 I was drunk from the drink that it mixed in me, the sweet sound of its lyre, / and I went while my mind trembled / from the bowl of its wisdoms.

Sweet drink filled my mind / and I moved away after I drank, / which mixed grace in it for me; / and left drink for others.

[749] I entered the banquet of its assembly, / for I was very thirsty for its sight, / 240 and from the flow of its words I was given drink, and my mind went exulting.

I entered its feast hungry, / for truth excelled there, / and with a medicine it met me there, / also deceit was reproached.

I saw the truth, which was seated / and that bird sings to [the truth] / and crowned in imitation of a king, / the sounds of praise with its harp.

245 I saw that diadem was bound with the truth, and a mute nature praises it; / 'Holy, Holy,' it cries out / to that one who was crucified upon a tree.

I saw that it was crowned with praises / and a nature deprived of words / like a bride of faith, / was singing rationally to it.

I saw that the truth was blurred there / 250 and glory was sprinkled like myrrh / by the songs of the bird, / and confession wafted there.

I saw that the sound wafted there of cane and crocus and cinnamon,
the truth of the true One and the Cross, for its hymns were poured out there.
I saw that from the unthinking mouth, chirping 'holy' and the truth,
but I understood that this Sign is of the one who changed water to wine.[15]
255 I celebrated and was drunk at its feast, for the Sign of Jesus had aroused it,
and in the assembly of its rational hymns, it was pleasing.
I saw the bird who knowingly arranged the words of (crying) holy,
and as if with delicacies I delighted in the meanings that doubled from it.
[750] I saw that the holy one was sanctified by a mouth deprived of words;
260 I was amazed at those who had strayed and did not desire (to cry) 'holy' with knowledge.

5. Praising the Only Begotten One

I abandoned my mind to the crowd, being pleased by its songs,
and I took an uncomprehending intellect, and I entered the exalted house.
I bowed down there to the Crucified one, who everyday performs new things,
and I praised him for his grace and his wise dispensations.
265 I praised and confessed his Cross, how much he desires the salvation of human beings,

for by all means he contrived to capture them for his glory.

I praised there his mercy which makes sinners truly alive,
and with staffs of wonder he chastises gently our humanity.

I praised him for as much as he endures the cruelty of our audacity,
270 everyday by his mighty deeds he truly admonishes our humanity.

I praised there his essence, whose wisdoms cannot be contained,
for the scribes are singing, and the natures concerning the Lordship that we have denied.

I praised him for his humility, for by it our humility was exalted,
and for his abundant renunciation, for by it our poverty became rich.

275 I praised him concerning his descent,[16] for by it our humanity was lifted up,
and about his conception and his birth,[17] for by it humanity gave birth to life.

I praised him concerning his swaddling clothes, for in them his glory is hidden,
and about that manger in which he lay,[18] for in it he made us sit down at the bridal feast.

---

[15] John 2: 1–11.
[16] Mt 1: 1–16.
[17] Mt 1: 18–19.
[18] Lk 2: 6–7.

I praised him for his upbringing,	for by it our infancy was reared,

280 [**751**] and about the milk that his mouth sucked, for by it he made us suckle his wisdom.

I praised him for he wished to live	under the law like a servant,
so that he might free all	by his mercy from the servitude of sin.
I praised him because he was circumcised,[19]	for by his circumcision he circumcised our iniquity,
and he cut off our old person,	and attached the new [person] in its place.
285 I praised him on account of his offerings,	which he went up to offer in the Temple,
and being that he is the high priest of truth,	he made himself the offering.
I praised him, the richest of all,	for he came to enrich the poor;
and chose for himself a poor mother,	she who was enriched by its truth.
I praised the one who bore all,	for wings and hands bore him,
290 and he came with his mercy to renew	the work which his hands had formed.
I praised him in the example of Simeon,[20]	and on account of his hands my mind extolled him,
for the hands of a human bore	that one who had borne the heights and the depths.
I praised the one loving all	who fled from Herod,[21]
his Sign chasing away the demons,	and hastening the watchers in heaven.
295 I praised him because	he lived under the subordination of parents,[22]
for we confess threefold	the One Father bringing all into subjection.
I praised him because he sat	among the scribes and the sages,

and through his learning, they were enlightened, both of the generations through knowledge.[23]

I praised him because he is	without time and without beginning,[24]
300 and because he became embodied,	they wrote about him in years and in days.
[**752**] I praised him about his youth	without being changed to an old person,
for in him our humanity was rejuvenated,	since through iniquity its generations became old.
I praised him for he desired what is right,	his strength giving rest to the weary,
and he laboured by his love for our sake,	so we might be saved from the faults of debts.
305 I praised him because he was baptized,[25]	even though he was holy in his nature,
for he gave birth to some so that they might become	pure children for God.

[19] Lk 2: 21.
[20] Lk 2: 33–35.
[21] Mt 2: 13–15.
[22] Lk 2: 51.
[23] Lk 2: 41–50.
[24] Jn 1: 1–3.
[25] Mt 3: 13–17; Mk 1: 9.

I praised him because of his fasting,[26]   in order to nourish all by his mercy,
for through it he recompensed for that   of fruit that had killed our generations.[27]
eating
I praised him because of his eating,   he was not lacking what he desired, yet was hungry,
310 for by it he gave his holy body to feed   to the hungry whom Satan had afflicted.
I praised him on account of his drinking,   the spring of all of our benefits,
for by it he gave to us the drink of his blood, which made those thirsty for error flee.
I praised him on account of his mortifications, for through them he gave us his virtues,
and on account of his sufferings and his scabs, for by them he mended our injuries.
315 I praised him because of his judgments,   judging all judges,
for by them he judged our enemy   and brought the ruler of the world to an end.
I praised him, the innocent one of all,   for he was scourged in the same way as the evil ones,
so that he might rescue humanity by his love   from the scourges of the Enemy.
I praised him who embraced the Cross by his mercy to give victory to all;
320 and like the Evil one, the evil ones mocked him, so that he might give royal blessings to us.
I praised him on account of his death,   for by it he distributed new life,
[753] for he has power over death and life,   so that through them he may administer benefits.
I praised him because of his freedom,   for he sat down among the dead in Sheol,
and by it he freed from within its pit   everyone that was subjected to corruption.
325 I praised him because of his resurrection,[28] for by it our mortality was resurrected;
Death and Satan died by it,   for they had killed our humanity.
I praised him for his ascension,[29]   by it we ascend to heaven,
so that we might become heirs there   in the indestructible kingdom.
I praised him for his virtue,   for by the right hand of his begetter,
330 our virtue was exalted,   for death pulls us down by corruption.
I praised him for his benefits,   for how they are defiled by some,
and for his blessings and his delights,   for they are defrauded by deniers.
I praised him for his humble ways,   which multiplied and gave to us a high estate,
and for the high estates of his essence,   which are falsely slandered by the arrogant.
335 I praised him for his wisdoms,   for by them he labours to capture us,
and for his deep meanings,   for by them he wishes to stir us up.

---

[26] Mt 4: 1–2.
[27] Gen 3: 1–19.
[28] Mt 28: 1–10; Mk 16: 1–15; Lk 24: 1–8; Jn 20: 1–18.
[29] Mk 16: 19; Lk 24: 51; Acts 1: 9.

I praised him on account of his powers, and for the riches of his fortitude,	for by them he strengthens our minds, for through them he fortifies our knowledge.
I praised him for his signs,	which he has placed in the natures and in books,[30]
340 so that by them he might chastise our humanity, lest it rebel against his Lordship.	
I praised him for all these things, [754] for a bird's voice had chastised me,	to crown all with his knowledge, that praised his majesty even more.
For the mind had become drunk	with the wonder and glory it had encountered,
and he reclined with thanksgiving,	and was pleased with its delicacies.

6. *The Parrot as the Sign/Rēmzā*

345 In the city which I saw a new, a mouth which spoke in a new way	joyfully, I had seen something new, a new glory for the Son.
In the city, which I saw for the first time, for I heard that it affirmed the truth	I enjoyed a new banquet, by language for the first time.
It affirmed the true things by hearing, *350* and like an infant at the breast of his mother,	dispatching a voice for the first time, I have drunk from its drink.
In the city, which I saw for the first time, I entered to praise the truth	the truth let loose in me its springs; in that church that Simeon had built.[31]
Then, by the wonder of the sight, I praised God all the more,	a decision was stirred up in me; for even a bird has praised him.
355 Zeal fermented in me even more for even the bird had proclaimed [faith]	to speak the faith, with the sweet sound of its songs.
My mind pushed me all the more, by hearing the voice of the bird	for it shouted my words in truth, who spoke words of truth.
It judged my being even more,	for it proclaimed the glory of the Crucified One,
360 by the bird's voice who gave praise	that the Crucified one was of God.
It pressed me all the more (to cry) Holy for the bird (cried) 'Holy, Holy';	to the Holy One, for in him All is holy, trumpeting his crucifixion.
[755] I thought even more, for it proclaimed for the death of the Crucified endures,	about life without death, which the bird also proclaimed.
365 I trembled more that it had preached for it is by weakness he was triumphant,	the powerful one and not the mortal, and the bird also praised him.

---

[30] The seven signs of Jesus in the Gospel of John.
[31] The Church of St. Peter in Antioch.

I hastened all the more to ask	for the pity and mercy of his essence,
for even a fowl by the sound of its songs	requested mercy from him.
I was stirred up, therefore, by wonder	due to the voice of the bird,
370 for it wove praise with truth,	and offered [praise] to the Crucified one of God.
It wove the songs like seals	in the pure gold of truth,
and brought to the Lord a diadem,	which the Crucified endured for the sake of for all.
It wove the songs like beads	with the jewels of true things,
and proceeded to offer it to the Crucified one,	for the natures cried out his glory.
375 It forged the true jewels	before the calf of faith,
and with joyous hymns, it extended out	the diadem of virtues to the Crucified one.[32]
It forged praise with thanksgiving	through wise hymns;
and proceeded to offer it to the Crucified one,	for he is the Lord of glory.
It wove again a diadem of praises,	with attractive seals of (crying) Holy,
380 and offered it to him to consecrate all,	for he sacrificed himself for our sakes.

7. *The Learning of a Child and the Learning of the Parrot*

Through these things, therefore,	the stirring of justice provoked us all the more,
for it raised its voice of truth,	and with it rebuked the wicked.
For the argument was not small	for those discerning, if they seek it;
since the bird by the words 'Holy'	proclaimed the faith.
385 [756] The sign is this and not less,	for [the bird] came to rebuke the audacious,
and the truth which its mouth chirped	chases contention far away.
Its voice, which its harp proclaimed, was sent for reproof,	
whether from learning,	or from the Sign of God.[33]
If it is his own learning,	this means it gave it so that you may learn;
390 and if it is a gift from His Sign,	see, the power of His mercy is revealed.
If someone taught the bird	that God is perception,
for it makes ascend not a few names	by the compositions of the words of praise.
If a rational human being	disputes with learning,
why did the bird not wonder,	for its songs chirp the answers?
395 The style is very difficult,	even to rational human beings,
until instruction enters	and places wisdoms in the soul.
Until a teacher is mightily moved,	and puts on fury and threats,
and through fear and terror	places examples in the soul.

---

[32] The previous three couplets depict a reversal of the Golden Calf, Ex 32.
[33] *Rēmzā*.

A tutor presses him, and raises the rod for his discipline,
400 and then opens the senses of his intellect to receive teaching.

He slaps his cheeks threateningly, and tears out the locks of his hair,
and then his mind becomes flexible, in order to speak the inflection of (his) words.

He offers his back to the pillar [for scourging], as well his sides to the whips,
and then he understands how to determine the knowledge of their concepts.

405 His body is full with bruises and swellings rise up on him,
and then he becomes malleable to accept the aphorisms in their differences.

[757] He grabs his neck and drags him, and pulls the ears of the youth,
and then he becomes malleable to discern the principles and inner treasures of knowledge.

He brings him as if to a furnace, and pours discipline into him,
410 and then being obedient, he pours a seal of learning upon his mind.

Through sufferings and torments, he refines and chastens him with abuses,
and then [the student] adopts the image in himself of knowledge and of meaning.

If a human being becomes malleable in this way towards learning;
how did the bird without bruises learn the compositions?

415 If a rational human being, knowledgeable and discerning,
contends routinely like this with scribes and with learning,

How much indeed will he be surprised by this bird full of wonder,
for without punishments and bruises, it chirped a composition of words.

[The Sign] gave guidance to this bird's chirping,
420 for without, it would not have been able to sing this composition.

Its action is through the Sign on every side so that one may look at it,
for my own mind thus perceived that it is a sign of reproof.

For the bird chirped the teaching of each thing,
and called out as if it were possible for something cooked and for drinks.

425 It chirped short names which were easy to speak,
in order to narrate the story that had been told by the ancients.

8. How Can a Bird Speak a New Song?

But a bird such as this? A bird has never spoken,
yet I have not heard (anything like) this, not even from a person have I received it.

[758] This is a new idea, which was heard from a bird,
430 for also time will confirm the demonstration of its unbelief.

This is a new confession which was uttered by a bird,
for it came to reprove humanity, lest they seize it with great care.

It is a new song that was proclaimed,
so that those who rejected

435 This is a new harp
and the crown that it weaves from them

This is new which was proclaimed,
and wove the truth of faith

This is a new idea,
440 and with portions of compositions,

Holy, Holy God,
for the Cross endures for our sake,

By (crying) Holy, the rejoicing of the seraphim
and the thanksgiving of the Holy Church

445 Just as the praise of the angels
In the same way, the church's praise

Just as the praise of the true ones
the Almighty and immortal one,

[The bird] offers (crying) 'Holy' with its tongue
450 and asks for mercy from there

for faith is speaking,
the faith of the Crucified One might be despised.

that stirs up 'Holies' by its songs,
stretches out to the Crucifixion.

for the bird shouted out 'Holy,'
for the glory of the church.

for it sang praise with its inflections,
it intoned confession by (crying) Holy.

almighty and immortal,
its tongue trumpeting wondrously.

always purifies its tongue,

the harp plays its hymns.

cries out 'Holy' to the Crucified one,
by which the immortal was crucified.

cries out that God is crucified,
who died for he wished to give life to all.

for the crucifixion of God,

like the church of saints.

9. Rebuke of Deniers of the Addition to the Trisagion

[759] Indeed, let the deniers be ashamed
for look, even a bird has chirped

Let them also be corrected by this
for look, the bird chirps it,

455 Let them be ashamed by the voice,
for they rejected something,

Let them be admonished by the silent one,
and weaving 'Holy' and praise and truth,

Let them be admonished by the bird
460 and by its words like a scribe

Let them be ashamed by the spreading of its wings, which depict the mysteries of the Cross,
and by its gentle words,

by the voice that proclaimed Holy,
that it is the crucifixion of God.

confession, for they have forgotten its power,
so that by it, [the bird] rebuked their minds.

which by its nature does not have speech,
look, its tongue sings.

for see, it confesses like someone rational;
offering to the Crucified one.

who has administered the mysteries of the Cross,
teaches and offers admonition.

by which it recites the faith.

10. The Bird as the Image of the Cross

Let the deniers who maligned the truth be embarrassed by the bird,
for in hidden and public matters, the glory of the Crucified one is inscribed on it.
465 When it spread out its wings it depicted the beautiful image of the Cross,
and when it opened its mouth it chirped its faith and its truth.
It is not afraid of the rulers, for you defile the voice of truth,
and is not favourable to the presence of teachers, for it speaks according to its will.
Authority does not frighten it, nor does majesty put it to shame;
470 for the confession, which its mind received, makes its tongue reply and give forth.
Many things do not upset it, so that it might be silent from its teaching,
for when the crowd presses towards it, the more its tongue sings.
[760] It is not contrary like a human being, so that it would change the word of its confession,
for it sings candidly to everyone according to its will.
475 If a teacher comes who is doubtful about the confession of its words,
[the bird] does not accept to be silent or to change its word.
It maintains a single confession in the mind which its Creator gave to it,
and through praise and the words (crying) 'Holy,' trumpeting it freely.
If gold should remain quietly in front of it, it does not change its confession,
480 for it does not consider gold anything regarding the learning it holds.
If silver increases and remains quietly, it looks at it despicably;
do not be persuaded to silence its harp from praise.
If you should toss to it pearls and jewels, instead of crumbs,
do not think you will silence it from the praise of the Crucified one.
485 If you offer emeralds and gems, instead of grains for its food,
you would not convince it to be silent from (crying) 'Holy' which its mouth chirps.
If you should draw a sharpened sword and flash it threateningly before it,
you would not frighten it to be silent from the glory, which provokes it.
If you should draw a bow against it, it is not afraid so as to relent to you,
490 and the sound of its songs is not silenced concerning the praise of the Crucified one.
If you threaten it with fire, you may destroy its beautiful appearance,
but you would not convince it to be silent a single day from its praising.
If you should aim a spear against it and speak with it angrily,
it does not keep silent concerning the praise, which its tongue has learned to chirp.

495 [761] If you should threaten all kinds of torments, it does not recognize your fame,
and the knowledge that its intellect has received does not muffle its tongue.

Curses do not stir it, and neither is it overcome by disturbances,
for it would be unfaithful to the Crucified one, as humanity is being saved by him.

If you would make perches of gold, instead of the perches on which it sits,
500 it is not persuaded to change a single[34] step of its learning.

Sitting on perches of wood it recites verses of the scriptures,
and if the king himself gives heed to it, it is not ashamed of its learning.

From the ancient and the new, the perch of its learning is repaired,
and the complete truth in its unanimity is solemnly restored by it.

505 The truth of the church in unanimity, its tongue chirps wondrously,
and securely maintains it, and does not keep silent about its confession.

Holy, Holy, God, its tongue imitates and chirps,
the verse that Isaiah wrote, in which the seraphim (cried) 'Holy.'[35]

The almighty and immortal one who was crucified and killed for our sake;
510 the verse that was written in the Gospel, sang the revelation of the apostles.

11. Do Not Exchange Anything for Faith and Truth

Come, be ashamed, O rational ones, by this talking fowl,
and openly speak and proclaim about the truth of the crucifixion.

Do not be ashamed of time, and do not let authority frighten you,
for time and authority pass away, yet the Crucified God lives.

515 Do not be terrified by the teachers, lest you receive great judgment
[762] from that teacher of teachers who judges the great and the small.

Do not let a gift entice you, to renounce the gift of life;
nor let honour entice you and you reject the suffering of Jesus.

Do not place the wealth of something over the wealth of the Crucifixion;
520 nor should a possession be counted [equal] with the possession of truth.

Do not exchange a pearl for the perfection of faith,
nor with gems nor with bdellium, nor with precious beads.

Do not exchange silver and gold for the truth of faith;
for if you acquire the entire world, it will be lighter than your riches.[36]

525 Do not exchange the degrees of glory for a degree that passes away like vapor;
and do not renounce the king of kings for authority that is like a shadow.

Do not be enticed by comforts, and renounce the wealth of afflictions;
love the sufferings of the Crucified one, rather than the pleasures of impiety.

---

[34] Lit., 'a full step'.
[35] Isaiah 6: 2–3.
[36] Cf. Mk 8: 36.

Neither by a little, nor by a lot, / should you lose the grip of truth,
530 lest it loses hold of you, / and you fall into a chasm of fire.[37]

Do not, my son, renounce the truth, / neither by a little, nor by a lot,
lest from your hands you are deprived / of the living seal of the kingdom.

Do not close the eyes of your mind / from the protection of faith,
for as its demonstration is virginity, / in an instant, it is stolen.

535 Do not become a friend / of one who is doubtful about the truth,
lest you also be in doubt / concerning the salvation that rescues you.

Do not enact love and mystery / with one who is crafty with his truth,
(763) lest you learn from his ways, / and travel on the path of his iniquity.

Do not let your mind be confused / with what corrupts his mind,
540 lest your ways are corrupted / by a series of his snares.

Do not allow knowledge to be thrown down [to others], / which is doubtful about God,
lest you are thrown down by God / and there is no way to break your fall.

Do not desire the ways / of one who ignores the truth,
for his roads make us go directly / to a chasm of flame.

545 Never journey on his path, / for his path descends to Sheol,
and his steps make us go directly / into the inner chamber of darkness.

Do not love one who is impure, / lest you become impure like him,
and do not cling to someone wicked, / lest he makes you taste his evil.

Do not incline your ear to a doubter, / neither a little, nor a lot,
550 for if you should serve his will, / you shall be a denier just like him.

If you love his company, / you shall share in his portion,
and if you do his will, / he shall drag you down to his torment.

Anyone who assists a murderer / inherits torment with him;
and whoever conceals an adulterer / has a share in his deed.

555 Whoever eats with a thief, / endures afflictions with him;
and whoever conceals plunder / pays back losses with him.

Whoever conceals brigands, / takes merchants captive with them,
and whoever conceals murderers, / disposes of corpses with them.

(764) By every evil thing to which you extend your hand, you have a share in its doing,
560 and every evil that occurs in you, / you are half of its share.

Distance yourself from evil ones, / if you love the truth,
and do not become a helper to them, / if you are helping yourself.

If you love faith, / do not love doubt,
for it is not possible to maintain at the same time light with darkness.

---

[37] Cf. Mt 17: 15, Mk 9: 22.

565 If you love God, / reject the side of Satan,
and if you hate falsehood, / proclaim the truth openly.
If you are refuting deceit, / cry out the truth like a trumpet,
and as for the side of falsehood, / refute and reject [it] as someone truthful.
It is not possible with two sides / to be an architect and builder,
570 for if you are building one side, / you are ruining the other side.
It is not possible for you to build deceit, / and to build truth along with it,
for the same spring does not flow / sweet and bitter water.
Despicable darkness does not persist / along with rays of light,
for unless the sun's reflections have set, / darkness has no power.
575 Do not show what is from true things, / while you are being held back by false things;
proclaim openly the truth, / if you are a truthful person.
If you seize beautiful and simple truth / by craftiness,
do not hold on to iniquity through truth, / and the truth through falsehood.
Do not show two faces, / so that you may agree with the victorious side,
580 [765] while a lie inhibits you / through the tricks of the deceitful.
Do not approach God / with cunning acts like Satan,
lest any cunning things be established / before God, as it is written.
Do not err in faith, / for its vision depends upon God,
lest your cunning acts rebel against him, / lest Gehazi rebels with his cunning [acts].[38]
585 Do not hide the path of your knowledge / from that One [who] sees hidden things;
reveal before the Lord your ways, / that is, paving your paths.
Do not exchange the truth for gold, / nor sell your faith,
lest you inherit the noose / of Iscariot the murderer.[39]
Do not stray in truth, / lest you inherit the leprosy of Gehazi,
590 Do not ignore the anathema of truth, / lest you besiege its obstructing barrier.
Do not stray like Ananais, / lest you expose yourself before the church,[40]
and do not hide deceit inside yourself, / lest it be exposed to the eye of the sun.
Do not approach the faith of the Cross, / from two sides,
lest you be uprooted from salvation, / like the People from its inheritance.

---

[38] 2 Kings 5: 20–27.
[39] Mt 27: 3–5.
[40] Acts 5: 1–11.

12. Do Not Lose Faith

595 Love the truth, my son, and reign,
do not obscure its precious seals

Extol it upon your lips,

embrace it lovingly,

Pour out its seal upon your mind,
600 and trample upon all afflictions,

[766] Prepare your soul for confinement,
and do not let the sound of your harp cease

Arm yourself against the sword
and do not cease from the battle

605 Fight until death
and do not show (your) back and turn away

Put on strength like a warrior
and tread the battles for its sake,

Put on love like a breastplate,[41]
610 and fight steadfastly,

Grab the spiritual sword in your hand, and encounter one with a schism,
and the spear head of the Cross,

Draw the bow of prayers
and shoot into the side of error,

615 Put on the [shoes of] readiness of the Gospel,[43] and trample the goads of the left,
and humble Satan and his ranks

With the whole armour of God,[44]
and be crowned with the truth,

Since your life is redeemed by the Crucified one, you are in debt to God the Crucified;
620 openly proclaim his truth

You are eating the sacrifice of his body;
[767] proclaim his truth openly

and place it like a diadem on your head;
from the eyes and from hearing.

so that it will place its necklace upon your neck;

so that it sets you upon its chariot.

and its money upon your tongue,
and do not cease from its praise.

and set yourself for torments,
from praise of the Crucified one.

with the living word of God,
on the side of faith.

for the sake of the victory of truth,
from a companion of faith.

in the company of faith,
if you are a disciple of the Crucified.

and put on a helmet of salvation,[42]
and do not surrender your faith.

which makes the ranks of paganism bow down.

with the select arrows of redemption,
and make its servants bow down before [faith].

by the name of the Crucified one.

dress steadfastly,
as you fight against deceitfulness.

until you earn his love.

you owe the sacrifice of your body,
until you turn to his reward.

---

[41] Eph 6: 14.
[42] Eph 6: 17.
[43] Eph 6: 15.
[44] Eph 6: 11, 13.

For when you drink from his side,[45] you owe the blood of your being,
speak about faith until you swallow its spear.

625 By the fastening of nails, you are freed from the chains of paganism,
you are indebted to the nails of the for by them he redeems you from error.
Crucified One,

You are redeemed by bitter and sweet, and you owe the reward on account of them,

drink suffering with the bitter, and do not let not your word cease from the truth.

You are honored by the precious blood of God who suffered for your sake,
630 your blood is little compared to his, immeasurable and incomparable.

You are bought by what is similar of his murder, for there is no water in their blood;
openly proclaim your salvation, until the killing of your self.

Fix on to it the hands of your mind by the faith of the Crucified one,
until the cutting off of your members, do not withdraw your hands from it.

635 Follow it and travel on its roads, and may its strength gird up your loins,
and do not be afraid, even if you travel in the valley of the shadows of death.[46]

13. *A Cloud of Witnesses*

You have superlative companions in the fellowship of faith;
adopt their wise examples, and be encouraged concerning the struggle.

Investigate their triumphs, and adopt the example of their ways of life;
640 and strive hard in their struggles, and be crowned with their crowns.

By faith Abel died, for by [faith] he presented his offering,
(768) die proclaiming your word, and your blood shall cry out like his own.[47]

By faith Enoch, who was crowned by [faith]'s virtue, was taken away;[48]
put on his virtue and be crowned, and set forth from there to the kingdom.

645 By faith Noah was delivered, a pleasing one in an evil generation;[49]
be triumphant in his truth, and defeat through it the wrathful deluge.

By faith the ark was constructed,[50] by which by [faith] was delivered;
proclaim faith, and it will shelter you like the ark.

---

[45] Jn 19: 34.
[46] Ps 23: 4a.
[47] Gen 4: 8, 10.
[48] Gen 5: 24.
[49] Gen 6: 9.
[50] Gen 6: 14–16.

By faith Abram left	family and lineage and neighbors;
650 you, leave brothers and relatives,	and follow [faith] and journey in a strange land.[51]
By faith, Abraham	was sufficient to receive the Promise;[52]
You, love faith,	and become an heir in the kingdom.
By faith, Abraham	offered his only son;[53]
take hold of faith,	and offer yourself for its sake.
655 By faith he was encouraged,	and he drew his knife over his son;[54]
be encouraged by [faith]'s truth,	and condemn and despise the sword.
By faith Isaac was handsome,	a living sacrifice, and he was crowned;
You, put on [faith]'s beauty as a sacrifice,	which is alive to God in his truth.
By faith, he opened	for his sheep a spring for drinking;[55]
660 you, open a fountain of truth	for the sheep, you have been redeemed by the Cross.
By faith, he prevailed	and defeated enemies;
You, prevail by [faith]'s truth,	and defeat and purge schismatics.
(769) By faith he sowed in the field,	and its seed came up two-fold;[56]
You, sow the word of truth,	for you will find harvests of salvation.
665 By faith, also Sarah	received the seed of the Promise;
You, by [faith] receive the promises,	and prevail over the illustrious.
By faith, she rebuked	Abimelech concerning his folly;[57]
You, by faith rebuke	the kings and priests for [faith]'s sake.
By faith, old age which was distinguished	was also rejuvenated;
670 you, become mature in truth,	and may its brightness conceal your countenance.
By faith, also Rebecca	betrothed her soul to the only [son];[58]
You, by faith, betroth	your soul to the Son, the Only Begotten.
By the love of Isaac, [faith] placed	bracelets and wrist jewelry upon her hands;[59]
You, by the love of the Only Begotten,	accept the bonds and nails upon your hands.
675 By faith, she filled the water,	and gave drink to the thirsty;[60]
you, fill up the water of truth,	and give drink to the lambs of the Messiah.

[51] Gen 12: 4.
[52] Gen 12: 1–3.
[53] Gen 22: 6–8.
[54] Gen 22: 10.
[55] Gen 29: 10 – Jacob, not Isaac.
[56] Gen 26: 12.
[57] Gen 20: 1–18.
[58] Gen 24: 62–67.
[59] Gen 24: 22.
[60] Gen 24: 15–21.

By faith, Sarah and Rebecca, chaste women, were affirmed;
in a strange country, beloved of their husbands, and rejected kings and comforts.
By faith, you should love and proclaim the sufferings of the Cross;
680 and do not exchange insults, neither in degrees nor in comforts.
By faith, Jacob was disturbed, and departed to a foreign land;[61]
You, stow [faith] also in your provisions, and you shall return with great profit.
By faith he had acted cunningly, and seized the right of the first-born and departed;[62]
(770) you, take the right of the first-born of faith, and journey in imitation of him.
685 By faith, he was cleansed, and was worthy to see the ladder;[63]
by faith, be purified to see the riches of the Cross.
By faith, he turned over the stone from the mouth of the well;
you, turn over the stone of truth, and reveal the spring of salvation.
By faith, he uncovered the well, and gave drink to the sheep of Rachel;
690 you, uncover the mysteries of truth, and give drink to the sheep of the church.
See the faith of Jacob who rebuked by [faith] one of the house of Laban;
and you, become light and rebuke the idolatry of graven images.
He did not regard favorably his neighbors, nor his parents, nor his fathers-in-law,
but by his faith, he confuted and rebuked and admonished the others.[64]
695 By faith, he lifted up the rods, for by them he designated the sheep,
and it gave birth to white spots and speckled ones for the admonition of his oppressors.[65]
By faith, lift up the rod of the Cross for the sheep,
and by sores on his body, [faith] will produce and engender praise.
By faith he wrestled, and defeated the spiritual man;[66]
700 by faith, wrestle and defeat the evil spirits.
By faith, his hands constructed and inscribed the Cross;
by faith, construct your entire self for the Cross.
By faith Joseph also was triumphant in his contests;
by faith, wrestle and win the battles of the deceitful one.
705 (771) By faith, he reproved his brothers before their father;[67]
by faith, reprove neighbors along with foreigners.

---

[61] Gen 29: 1.
[62] Gen 27: 1–45.
[63] Gen 28: 10–17.
[64] Gen 29–31.
[65] Gen 30: 25–43.
[66] Gen 32: 24.
[67] Gen 37: 2, 5–11.

By faith, he leapt into the pit,
proclaim [faith] and if you fall,
By faith, he defeated the fire,

710 and after all his struggles,
By faith take hold of

and upon a chariot of glory,
By faith, he was nourished
Abba and Lord and ruler

715 You, accept the demand of truth,
and satisfy those hungry for truth,
By faith, he commanded

for he believed in the resurrection,
By faith, accept
720 and through its proclamation make yourself
By faith, Moses rejected
and chose poverty for himself,
By faith, hold fast
more than all the treasures
725 By faith, Moses renounced,

and like a mother, he became a son
(772) By faith, he was bold
he reproved Hebrews, his [own] people,

Isaiah also raised his voice

730 faith taught him,
"Do not refrain from crying out,"
and by [faith]'s truth his voice shouted

and rose up from within the pit;[68]
[faith] will grab you and raise you up.
which encountered him in the inner chamber;[69]
he was driven about on a chariot.[70]
and trample upon the burning coals of afflictions,
you shall be carried into the kingdom.
and satisfied by affliction;
he became in Egypt and in [faith]'s kingdom.[71]
and gather in the storehouse of the Spirit,
and you will be praised in the kingdom.
that his bones should be brought out from Egypt,[72]
and in the judgment and the reward.
the truth, which is inscribed in the scriptures,
depart hence to heaven.

the treasures of the kingdom,
for he was a stranger with God.
and delight in and love its mortifications
and honours and principality.
lest he become a son of the daughter of Pharaoh,[73]
of faith, and departed to a foreign country.
and rejected the Egyptians;
whom he saw quarreling.[74]
(two folios missing)
by what was praiseworthy among the prophets;[75]
"Cry out at the top of your lungs."
[faith] advised the glorious one,
like a trumpet throughout the land.

---

[68] Gen 37: 23–8.
[69] Gen 39: 6–18.
[70] Gen 41: 43.
[71] Gen 41: 46–57.
[72] Gen 50: 25.
[73] Ex 2: 15b.
[74] Ex 2: 13–14.
[75] Isa 1: 1–4.

He dared to speak openly against a people who had silenced the prophets,
and proclaimed the glory of the Crucified one by that mystery of apostleship.
735 He chastised the tribes with the Nations about the mystery of Emmanuel,
and chastised the kings and rulers on account of his faith.
With a wooden saw they cut him, but he did not cut off his voice from [faith's] word,[76]
for even as he descends, see, he cries out and proclaims the faith.
By faith Jeremiah raised up his voice among the People,
740 and put on a coat of afflictions, but did not abandon the excellence of his beauty.
He also placed his holy soul in chains and afflictions,
but did not keep silent about the word of truth, which was defiled by false ones.
He made his face like emery, and his forehead like brass,
and reprimanded the congregations of the People and the Nations concerning the truth.
745 (773) By faith he despised the false prophets,
and they beat and cast [stones] at him like a dog,[77] but he was not silent from preaching.
They threw him into a muddy pit,[78] but he was not silent from his lyre;
he ate bread with affliction, and did not discern his companion from its own.
By faith, Hezekiah tore down and dismantled the idols,[79]
750 and roused up the fear of God, according to the commandment of the law.
By [faith], he destroyed the idols and cut down the images of sin;
and restored the holy temple and celebrated worship like David.
By faith, he pacified that iniquitous Sennacherib,
and by [faith], fought with him and defeated him as if his camp were sheaves.[80]
755 By [faith], he humbled the threat and pride of Assyria,
and made kneel and destroyed its mighty men by the sword of his faith.
By [faith], he turned back the sun on high, while he prayed about his illness,[81]
and from the mouth of death, [faith] snatched him, and the sun returned to its glory.

---

[76] *Martyrdom and Ascension of Isaiah* 5:1–16; trans. M.A. Knibb, *The Old Testament Pseudepigrapha. Volume 2*, ed. James H. Charlesworth (Doubleday & Co.: Garden City, NY, 1985), 143–76.
[77] Lamentation 3: 53.
[78] Lam 3: 53.
[79] 2 Kings 18.
[80] 2 Kings 19.
[81] 2 Kings 20: 8–11.

By faith, he was crowned	with the crown of David his father,
760 and by the mysteries his beauty shone,	which faith had adorned him.
By faith, also Josiah the righteous	was illustrious,[82]

and by [faith], he was prosperous in his ways, and was glorified in holiness.

By faith, those of the house of Ḥananya	were triumphant in Babylon;[83]
and grace and compassion they found,	for they had honoured faith.

765 By [faith], those who fasted became wise, and by [faith] the righteous were crowned;
(774) and they reprimanded Nebuchadnezzar, the lion who tore apart mortals.[84]

By faith they were nourished	by grains instead of delicacies,
and instead of drinking wines,	[faith] strengthened their bodies by water.[85]
They were nourished by [faith] in everything,	and became valiant by its delicacies;
770 [faith] opened springs in their intellects	of wisdom and understanding.
By truth, they despised error,	and greatly rebuked doubt;

and they did not accept in the presence of rulers that their one ruler was a god.[86]

They rebuked the sages of Babylon,	who were not wise in the truth;
also, the Magi and sorcerers,	an assembly that was foreign to the truth.

775 They investigated by [faith] the depths, and revealed the secret things by [faith],
and stirred up with fear and wonder the king and his princes.

They were prepared against fire,	in order not to renounce faith,
and despised and disdained the sword,	so that it might not eliminate [faith's] wealth from them.
By faith, they were set on fire,	and a flame burned from them;[87]

780 and by [faith's] love they burned with zeal, and entered, despising the flame.

They despised the two furnaces	which burned for the sake of their annihilation;
they kindled in the fire one piece of wood,	and the heat burned the other.
They despised the idol of the king,	and the king just like his idol,
but honoured and worshiped God,	for honor is fitting to [God].

785 They despised the degrees and afflictions, and despised the kings and princes;
So that they gave their bodies as burnt offerings, lest they renounce faith.

---

[82] 2 Kings 22.
[83] Daniel 3.
[84] Daniel 3: 29.
[85] Daniel 1: 11–16.
[86] Daniel 3: 12.
[87] Daniel 3: 21–2.

(775) By the trust of [faith], they entered the furnace, and [faith] prepared a place before them,[88]
and summoned a fourth, who would make a couch in the fire.
He made [faith] a will and a sign, a watcher who carried refreshments,
790 and generated a breath of dew in that furnace of blazing fire.
The fire embraced their bodies in which faith dwells,
and went forth to kill those of error, who were calumniators of the steadfast.

14. By Faith, Daniel and the Prophets

By faith, the captive Daniel excelled;
he rebuked and admonished the kings and rulers and became wise by [faith].
795 He established [faith] as a crown of virtues, and by [faith] ruled over the kings;
and worship and incenses and offerings they offered to him, as if to God.
[Faith] opened in him interpretations and hidden riches of wisdoms,
and he enlivened and celebrated the vanquished, and defeated and killed the deceitful.
By faith, he won and was triumphant in two pits which they had dug for him;[89]
800 and the power of [faith]'s truth shut the mouth(s) of lions.
[Faith] made him desirable to the watchers and beloved among the angels,
and on the heights and the depths [faith] broadcast the exploits of his righteousness.
By faith the entire assembly of prophets was triumphant,
and they rebuked kings and princes and endured afflictions on account of [faith].
805 By faith, they adorned themselves and became spiritual temples;
And the Spirit which declared about Jesus filled them with the mysteries of salvation.
By faith, Mordecai and Esther were delivered from Haman,[90]
(776) and they delivered the People with them from the cunning acts of the deceptive one.
Esther put on faith and entered to [see] the king,[91]
810 and more than garments and jewelry, beauty and brightness clothed her.
[Faith] blossomed upon her face, and she was chosen by her companions;
and she took the crown and the kingdom, which faith had given to her.
By faith Mordecai, her friend, was strengthened against Haman,
as he had despised the servant, an unbeliever and full of pride.

---

[88] Daniel 3: 24–5.
[89] Daniel 6: 16.
[90] Esther 3: 1–15.
[91] Esther 5.

815 By [faith], he seized him by a net he had hidden, and by a snare he had hung, he trapped him,
and upon the wood which [Haman] wanted to crucify [others], the crucifiers crucified him to it.[92]

By faith also, the holy Ezekiel, was triumphant;
and multitudes of afflictions surrounded him, but he did not cut off his love from his [faith].

He ate bread by measure, and drank a small amount,[93]
820 and full of shameful deeds and afflictions, he did not pause and cease from [faith]'s course.

He sharpened his tongue like a sword, for he shaved his head and his beard with it,
and rebuked and admonished his people, and lifted up a sign before them.

He threatened the princes, and was forceful against the powerful,
and despised their idols by the zeal of faith.

825 By [faith], he was cleansed like light, and saw the throne of God,[94]
and the image of someone who was above it,[95] which was explained by Christ.

By [faith], he cried out about resurrection, and inscribed the Cross upon the bones,
while from the four corners, he summoned the Spirit to come.

By [faith], the church was revealed to him, which he compared with a torrent,
830 (777) also the mystery of the Crucifixion, which he inscribed on the building and the door.

He was an acute observer of [faith], and watched and kept its morning watch,
and like a horn he called out and proclaimed among his people concerning [faith's] honor.

15. *Rebuilding Jerusalem, by Faith*

By faith also, the illustrious Zerubbabel was crowned;
and he led and brought up from Babylon the People whose servitude was finished.[96]

835 By [faith], he was valiant like David, and repaired the breaches of his town,
and rebuilt a city that had been torn down, which had not honoured faith.

He rejoiced and settled his People, and Jerusalem was rebuilt by him;
and by faith, he raised up the place that paganism had torn down.

By [faith], he gathered his scattered People and dispersed the Nations who had attacked it;
840 and he rebuilt the torn-down walls, just as Jeremiah had prophesied.

---

[92] Esther 7: 1–10.
[93] Ezk 4: 16.
[94] Ezk 1: 26–27.
[95] Ezk 1: 28.
[96] Ezra 2: 2.

Like a wall, he repaired
and like a lion, he broke its enemies,
that People whom Babylon had torn down,
for faith emboldened him.

By faith, Joshua, son of Jozadak,
and he ordained the priesthood of Joshua,
was also crowned,[97]
like Zerubbabel, his kingdom

845 By [faith], his spirit was awakened,
and raised up the temple and sanctuary,
and he honored the holiness of his name,
and brought up its holy vessels.

By [faith], he supplied the holy sacrifice,
and he returned the holy vessels,
which the wicked nations had trampled,
which the Chaldeans had seized.[98]

By [faith], he renewed the holy altar
850 and according to the law which Moses had given, he performed the sacrifices of thanksgiving.
by vows and burnt offerings,

(778) By [faith], he subdued Satan
and an angel descended for his honor
who stood up to injure him on his right;
and rebuked his ill-wisher.[99]

With [faith]'s pure praise, he was honored,
and removed and cast away from himself
and dressed him with fine clothes;
the clothing that paganism had defiled.[100]

855 By [faith], he was purified like Aaron,
and administered the mysteries of the Son,
and put on the robes of priesthood,
and clothed himself with His name's brightness.

[Faith] crowned him with the crown
and with gold, which Jedaiah had given,
of blessings, which Tobit had offered,
and Huldai his companion, the offering.

As for Joshua, Joshua was emboldened,
860 and like Joshua, he subdued the Nations after he had gone up from Babylon.
and became a priest of God;

By [faith], he renewed and rebuilt the holy [sanctuary] that had lain wasted for seventy years;
and he arranged the holy vessels, which for years were absent from the sacrifices.

He reclaimed the place that had lain waste, and made in it a feast of sacrifices,
and renewed the holy mysteries, until Jesus his Lord came.

865 By faith Tobit as well as Jedaiah
and Huldai and Ezra and Nehemiah,
were celebrated,
who rebuilt the temple and the city.

By [faith] also, Simeon was renowned,
and he made the vestment shine
the pure and illustrious priest;
like the morning star from the sanctuary and veil.

By faith Zechariah, Judah,
870 and Eleazar was illustrious,
as well as Nahum, excelled,
for the kings judged him for [faith]'s sake.

---

[97] Ezra 2: 2.
[98] 1 Esdras 4: 57.
[99] Zechariah 3: 1–2.
[100] Zech 3: 4.

16. By Faith, Shmoni and her Sons

(779) By faith, Shmoni and Antiochus was wearied, and her illustrious sons were celebrated,[101] and did not cut them off from [faith's] love.

Martyrs who were prior to the Messiah but did not turn away from faith endured tortures and afflictions, to sacrifice and worship idols.

875 By [faith], they endured all afflictions, and wafting up and ascending lacerating tortures and amputations, from the fire as sweet aromas.

By [faith], they despised threats, and were prepared against the sword, and disdained and disregarded all disturbances, lest they renounce faith.

They kept the law of God, 880 and neither by a little nor by a lot and despised the tyrant's commandment; did they desire to disparage faith.

They honored [faith] by the suffering of their bodies, and by the amputation of their limbs;
and by the faith of God they did not deny [faith] before the deniers

[Faith] crowned them with crowns of glory among mortals, and they honored [faith] through afflictions, before the Nations as well as their kings.

885 They defeated the kingdom and error, and loved and adored the truth and possessed the taste of old age; [more] than transitory honors.

They became like the seven luminaries, for it made sprout the pure wings all of whom shone by the truth, of Shmoni, the holy candlesticks.

They shone like the days of a feast, 890 by the seven feasts of Shmoni, so that through them the sanctuary is adorned for [faith] wove the number of seven.

By faith, the seven holy clusters (780) in a vine full of glory, were strengthened and it yielded the land of the Law.

By faith, the sons of Shmoni and [faith] was crowned by its friends were crowned like lilies; like a crown of its seven blossoms.

17. By Faith, the Maccabees

895 By faith, Mattathias, full of exploits, he tore down the entrances of idols, was emboldened;[102] and rebuked the tyrannical king.

His hands grasped firmly onto God, and he rose up in the presence of all the People,

for he would not serve paganism, and would not worship error.

---

[101] 2 Maccabees 7.
[102] 1 Macc 2: 1–48.

[Faith] left an inheritance to the sons of his people when he slept with the upright;
900 he wrote [faith] and gave an inheritance to his sons through the covenant of his divisions.

By his life he honored [faith] and by his death, he made an offering for [faith]'s sake;
and [faith] adorned him and made him great, and celebrated him among the upright.

Judas Maccabeus the warrior	held on to faith,[103]
and as the most precious treasures	he weighed its holy riches.
905 He kept [faith] as a deposit,	and received it as wealth
from that illustrious father	who gave [faith] to him as an inheritance.

He girded himself with [faith] like a coat of mail, and like a shield he held [faith] in his hand;

and he fought until death,	lest he depart from its profit.
[Faith] broke the warriors before him,	and made the power of the tyrants fall down;

910 and with those few who accompanied him, he made bow down thousands and myriads.

[Faith] summoned the hosts to his aid,	and the cavalry of light surrounded him;
and in the time of faith,	they hovered over and shaded his head.
(781) By [faith], Judas and his valiant brothers were glorified and crowned;[104]	
Simeon also supported Joseph,	and Jonathan multiplied virtues.

915 All of them honoured [faith] in persecution, and lived with [faith] in afflictions;

in battle they died for its sake,	and did not allow a blemish in [faith]'s honor.

With [faith's] armour they fought against kings, and tore down and broke the strong,

and made mighty men tremble	by the valiant deeds they performed through [faith].
[Faith] cast fear of them upon thousands,	and made legions tremble by their voice;
920 and the kings were shocked and disturbed	by the pursuit of [faith]'s friends.
With crowns [faith] crowned them,	for its glory crowned them,
and put purples on them,	for they loved and adored [faith]'s promise.
[Faith] summoned kings to their exploits,	and they gave the right hand to the covenant,
and brought gifts and offerings	to the friends of faith.
925 By [faith], they were strengthened and emboldened	like the whelps of lions;
and [faith] silenced the roars	of the beasts of the pagans.
[Faith] broke the chariots of the kings,	and escorted them on (double) chariots;
and in victory [faith] tied	crowns as well as necklaces on them.

---

[103] 1 Macc 3–9.
[104] 1 Macc 10–16.

18. Understanding What the Bird Said

This cloud of thanksgiving surrounds you, O disciple;
930 be encouraged and travel with them in the company of faith.

This band of the illustrious went out to encounter the truth;
it was strengthened by their struggles, and it shall be crowned by their crowns.

With these legions, it hunted, for it died in battle for [faith]'s sake;
(*782*) you also should fight zealously for its triumphant victory.

935 This wall of the powerful, the wretched surrounds you, do not be afraid;
raise up your voice truthfully, and do not be shaken by the strong.

All these illustrious ones, and there are many more than these,
sensed the mysteries of the Crucified one, and became rich in the Trinity.

All of them endured afflictions for the sake of faith;
940 do not shrink from its temptations, for by them you may become beautiful as gold.

They tied all of them through afflictions to the crown of righteousness,
and by sufferings of all kinds, they gave praise by the same faith.

They testified by [faith] in all struggles, and persevered by [faith] in all generations;
they endured all deaths for [faith], and all conflicts for [faith's] sake.

945 Be encouraged and travel as well on this narrow road,
for at its end, the kingdom of all good things is a delight.

Do not love the wide road, for its end [leads] to Gehenna,
where it is crowded with torments, and the filth of a worm and darkness.

Restrict yourself and travel with afflictions, and by them you shall find pleasures;
950 do not travel with luxuries, for by them you will find miseries.

Do not let honors weaken you, and cast away the honor of the illustrious;
do not lower yourself to comforts, and destroy the blessing of the promises.

Narrow is the door of salvation, and whoever afflicts himself shall enter through it;
but if it is widened through comforts, its affliction drives it away.

955 By the measure of humanity it is the door that opens to the upright;
(*783*) do not think one who wears luxurious things is able to enter.

Do not become hardened by comforts, and put on the weight of possessions,
for that door cannot contain you through which the upright ones enter by afflictions.

The comfortable one remains outside of it, and only the afflicted one enters;
960 restrict your soul with afflictions, and you will inherit its blessings within.

19. The Afflictions of Being Born

Even the infant who comes to salvation
but if he does not suffer with afflictions,

If the pangs do not afflict him,
there he inherits darkness,

965 Strangled is the infant who does not sense
and he goes from darkness to darkness,

He treats his mother harshly by afflictions,
for he inflicts injuries on her and abandons

His advent is full of pain,
970 and mourning dresses his mother

In the same way, you should also look through
for if you do not pass through afflictions,

Mourning only bears you
for you have repaid [grace] evil rewards

975 All its virtues you have rejected,

for it has sealed you in the image of God,

(784) [Grace] bore you in the womb of life,
and pleased you by its creatures,

For not willingly does the fetus die
980 but your death is by your will,

Accompany the fetus as he goes,
in the same way that one went,

Live in virtuous ways,
and may your soul give birth with afflictions

985 Be very proud of its virtues,
on account of myriads which are better than this

Do not be strangled, O fetus,
lest your journey be for you

The life of the infant is the soul,
990 and the nourishment of the infant is milk,

passes through the door of afflictions;
he will not see the light that is here.

which had struck and bent over his mother,
in a place which is deprived of life.

the narrow door through which he must pass,
and vacant is his coming and going.

while he is deprived of benefits,
the iniquitous womb which bore him.

and afflictions without profit;
in his birth and in his mortality.

the door that gives birth to salvation,

your soul is strangled of life.

to grace which gives birth to you,
as you come to the end of life.

which it has lent to you, although you did not take;
and has given you the Spirit and salvation.

and the blessing of the mysteries suckled you,
but you saddened it by sorrow for your death.

in the womb of his mother,
and your life is by your will.

without sins and without reward;
for the wickedness of his will has killed him.

in the womb of your mother Grace,
to the world full of pleasures.

the world which shall come from this,
from within the womb of the mother.

in the womb full of life,
from darkness to darkness.

but yours is faith;
but yours is the body and blood.

The womb of the fetus is a womb of flesh,	but yours is a spiritual [womb];
its womb is in impure waters,	but yours is in holy [waters].
That one in a womb of blood pulsates,	but you are in the womb of baptism;
for that one's birth a womb of flesh,	but for you a spiritual womb.
995 For the fetus his birth is old,	but yours is new;
the birth of the fetus is of childhood,	but yours is of a mature person.
Your mind shall be reared in life,	for faith is breathed into it;
(**785**) do not lose your faith,	and lose your soul from salvation.

The body and the blood are your nourishment, for powerful is the work of God;
1000 and there is nothing that is able to prevail over you, if your will desires.

Tougher is your strength than Satan,	if you do not surrender yourself;
your life is superior to death,	if you do not kill yourself.
You shall defeat the bars of Sheol,	if you do not harm yourself;
you shall prevail over the gate of death,	if you do not allow your freedom to fail.
1005 Your strength is tougher than destruction,	if you guard yourself;
and your creation from desolation,	if you do not ruin your foundation.
You are a new human being,	if your will does not become old;
and life is superior to death,	if you do not die from the truth.

20. *In Praise of the Cross*

In the Crucified one, I have found these	virtues without number;
1010 you, preach his faith,	for even the bird declared it.
Although the Crucified was not for [the bird's]	sake, it chirped His praise and His truth,
since he was intended for you,	do not be silent from His praise.
That [bird] spoke about his redemption,	although it did not taste of his body;
you, give thanks for his redemption,	for you are eating his body and his blood.
1015 That [bird] sang of his holiness,	although it did not experience his forgiveness;
you, give thanks for his forgiveness,	for by his holiness you have been absolved.
That [bird] offered praise for his death,	although resurrection was not promised to it;
you, proclaim his suffering and his death,	for you are reveling in his life.

That [bird], who did not inherit his promises, was diligent to sing his praises;
1020 (**786**) as for you, everything he had, he gave to you, shout and proclaim his honors.

Something which the ear did not hear,	the sufferings of the Crucified one gave to you;
fill the ear from your sounds,	the words of faith.

Something which the eye did not see,
May it become a vision for sight,
1025 Something that did not ascend upon the heart,
may your heart become a spring of life,

Since he came to invite you to his bridal chamber, enduring sufferings for your sake;
make him the bridal chamber of your mind, and celebrate there his honor.

Because your ears heard his redemption, proclaim in [his] ears his confession;
1030 and because your eyes saw his mercy, show his humility to the eyes.

Since your heart is full of his promises, let us make his praises increase and abound;
and because your body saw his pardons, let there be for him a spoken sacrifice.

Since he gave to you the earth and heaven, what do you have to give to him?
His own person became your gift, what is the glory that you repaid to him?

1035 Accept the cup of salvation, and cry out in his name and affirm him;
and persevere until death, and do not lose his faith.

the death of the Crucified one gave to you;
and praise him before the judges.
the shame of the Crucified one gave to you;
and praise and proclaim his thanksgiving.

21. *The Crucified One as Bridge and Ladder*

In the Crucified one find life,
he is for you a bridge, so cross over
(787) In the Crucified one I found these,
1040 he guided us beyond death,

He became for you a ladder,
the Father and the Son testify to me,

Become for him a temple trumpet

and speak about his faith
1045 Become for him a true labourer,
about his miracles and redemptions,
Become for him a living trumpet,
for Jesus is the Lord of glory,

These things justice has promised us
1050 and I also promise these things to you,

and tread upon the neck of death;
to the light of the Trinity.
and the Holy Spirit testifies to me;

according to what he proclaimed by the prophet.

so that you might reach the higher life;
and the Spirit that chirped through the Apostles.

for the Crucified one who has increased your wealth;
with authoritative confidence.
who preaches from dawn to evening
and about his sufferings and humiliations.
who shouts and proclaims his honor,
who was nailed and crucified for your sake.

by the movements which grace gave;
O disciple of faith.

These things that you said, indeed you said, for I am speaking to you, as well as me with you;	
You speak, as I have spoken to you,	for just as you have spoken with me, I will speak to you.
Proclaim your word as you have heard,	for just as you have declared to us, I declare to you;
do not listen to the voice of a stranger regarding the report of life of the Scriptures.	
1055 Just as you called me so I should call you, for you should summon your self and others;	
and after the readings of the prominent ones, flee far away from his chasm.	
These examples you gave to me	from the examples of earlier upright ones;
(788) I also have given their examples to you,	so that you might observe the place of their joy.
From within the meadows of the scriptures,	you have given me a crown of blossoms,
1060 and its wreath with the virtues of the upright, so that you may be crowned in its truth.	
For I have recited to you about their virtues,	and about the incenses of their fragrances,
and may you be crowned with their crowns,	and retain their fragrances.
I gave you some of their colors,	and some of the blossoms of their ways of life,
and from the best lilies,	for their truth blossoms on earth.[105]
1065 I spoke to you although I was not adequate	for the great wealth of the ancients;
and I speak and am not adequate,	concerning the treasures of the last ones.
I have admonished you by what is old,	and I shall also [do so] with the new;
be alert and sing with me glory	to the Father and the Son and the Holy Spirit.

The end of the *mēmrā* about that bird who chirped "Hagios O Theos" in the city of Antioch, which was written by Mar Isaac.

---

[105] Cf. Mt 6:28–29.

CHAPTER 3

Interpretative Essay: Becoming Parrot—Voice's Subject Formation

Abstract This chapter provides an interpretative framework for approaching broad implications of the late fifth-century sermon of Isaac of Antioch on the parrot who told him the correct position to take in the contemporary theological controversy of the Addition. It gives a contextualized summary of the sermon, and then it draws out the connections of Isaac's sermon with a long history in western and eastern traditions of seeing parrots as quasi- or alter-humans. Capacities of speech and mind have very often marked the threshold separating the human and the animal, and that threshold is very often blurred when parrots are involved, just as Isaac discovered in his sophisticated sermon. The result is a strikingly modern, poetic reflection on animality and the divine.

Keywords Isaac of Antioch • Addition controversy • Syriac Christianity • Parrots and animal studies • Media studies

> We see nature and attempt to illuminate its obscurities, without hearing the voice that fills the universe, sky and earth, climate and storms, springs and wind, the tumult of the tides, the trembling of the poplars, the genesiac heat of the beasts, the murderous or fervent noise of men gathered together, the imploring prayer of love.

© The Author(s), under exclusive license to Springer Nature Switzerland AG 2024
R. A. Kitchen, G. Peers, *The Bird Who Sang the Trisagion of Isaac of Antioch*, Palgrave Studies in Animals and Literature,
https://doi.org/10.1007/978-3-031-60077-7_3

Hear, O Israel. 'Ephphatha': be opened (Deut. 6:4, Mark 7:34). Has human knowledge, consciously or out of respect, left this path of listening exclusively to religion?[1]

Traditionally, commentators on relations between human and animals in Late Antiquity have fallen back on the normative position most dramatically enacted in Adam's naming of the creatures: here is the primal moment in which the human—and a single figure at that!—sorts and dominates all the non-human creatures (see Gen. 1:26).[2] This 'instinct' for classify-and-command initiated at the beginning of sacred history has deeply informed western history. Yet there has always been pushback and probing of it in texts and images, in every period. Here our concern is with Late Antiquity. Patricia Cox Miller has recently examined the sets of relations that vacillated between this rhetoric of domination and what she calls "the zoological imagination."[3] As she writes, Late Antique writers frequently "think both *about* and *with* animals, especially in terms of their emotional, ethical, psychological, and behavioral continuities with human beings." Isaac of Antioch's fifth-century metrical sermon "The Bird Who Sang the Trisagion" belongs to this same world so vividly evoked by Miller, a world where the human probes *itself* through animals, where deep affinities are found, and where new becomings are possible.

For Isaac, language is the primary point of continuity between human and animal. Isaac finds truth and salvation in parrot speech, and if the parrot's inferior command of language and mind, but also lack of sin, is an implicit limiting factor for participation in salvation,[4] Isaac reveals himself remarkably open to parrot superiority. He also finds himself falling into a kind of parrot-hood himself, as he repeats and mimics the words of the

---

[1] Michel Serres, "Epilogue: What Hearing Knows," in *The Re-Enchantment of the World: Secular Magic in a Rational Age*, ed. Joshua Landy and Michael T. Saler, trans. Trina Marmarelli (Stanford: Stanford University Press, 2009), 259–73, 351, here 273.

[2] See the beautiful counterpoint in Ursula Le Guin, "She Unnames Them," *New Yorker* (21 January 1985): 27.

[3] Patricia Cox Miller, *In the Eye of the Animal: Zoological Imagination in Ancient Christianity* (Philadelphia: University of Pennsylvania Press, 2018), here 4.

[4] For an argument that places animals back in the salvific plan, see Daniel P. Horan, "Deconstructing Anthropocentric Privilege: Imago Dei and Nonhuman Agency," *Heythrop Journal* 60, no. 4 (2019): 560–70, as well as David M. Carr, "Competing Construals of Human Relations with 'Animal' Others in the Primeval History (Genesis 1–11)," *Journal of Biblical Literature* 140, no. 2 (2021): 251–69.

bird who showed him the way to truth. Here Isaac appears to share the position of older writers like Plutarch and Porphyry, who were willing to ascribe *logos*, or reason/speech, to animals, and thereby skirted the anthropocentrism that has marked animal writing at least since Aristotle.[5] In the influential view of the latter, animals are irrational and therefore are definitively lesser in comparison to humans.

In these ways, Isaac emerges as a writer many of us now might feel real sympathy with, in his receptiveness to animals' agency and his embrace of "the pensivity of animals as fellow creatures in a shared world."[6] As the epigram above by the French philosopher Michel Serres evokes, Isaac was able to listen truly in his faith. As if responding to those invocations of Deuteronomy and Mark, he was opened to the animal voice; he heard and was deeply transformed.[7] His sermon is an attempt to open his audience similarly to parrot, as they find their salvation through the assumption, quite literally, of animal speech. 'Normal' positions are productively reversed: parrots, who are assumed to mimic, speak divine truth, and humans, who are assumed to have superlative reason, repeat after the wise creature, led by Isaac's example. In this way, personhood as a human category is redefined, as its exclusive humanness is undermined.[8]

This chapter argues for a merging of human and parrot natures in Isaac's text. The sermon is an extended analysis and self-analysis in how

---

[5] Miller, *In the Eye of the Animal*, 86–98.

[6] Miller, *In the Eye of the Animal*, 91.

[7] Or in the words of Vinciane Despret, "Inhabiting the Phonocene with Birds," in *Critical Zones: The Science and Politics of Landing on Earth*, ed. Bruno Latour and Peter Weibel, trans. Chris Turner (Karlsruhe: ZKM-Cambridge, MA: MIT Press, 2020), 255, "Inhabiting the Phonocene certainly means trusting in the musicality of the world (and its rumblings) and attempting to learn from them; it means leaving the sphere in which the *logos* of the *anthropos* is exclusively privileged, in order to speak once again with those that are other than human."

[8] For useful parallels for a way to expand our notions of Late Antique 'being', see Mel Y. Chen, "The Gate and the Unreachable," in *Lin May Saeed: Arrival of the Animals*, ed. Robert Wiessenberger (Williamstown, MA: Sterling and Francine Clark Art Institute, 2020), 93–103, here 99, "…for many indigenous people and cultures of relational knowledge, personhood is a feature of being that is not reducible to species, or even biological notions of life; one can recognize the personhood of stone, rivers, mountains, and understand them as agentive." For a comparable argument based in Late Antiquity, see Glenn Peers, *Animism, Materiality and Museums: How Do Byzantine Things Feel?* (Leeds: ARC Humanities Press, 2021).

alike human and animal are, and in how profoundly these natures can interchange and mingle, leaving each transformed. We don't have the parrot's perspective, since Isaac doesn't try to imagine how they felt after they spoke to Isaac, but we do know the human aftermath, in Isaac's adopting the sacred truth of the parrot's position.[9] Isaac is certainly never the same, and if his text was persuasive (which is easy to believe), neither was his audience. Friedrich Nietzsche's deeply evocative call might be apposite here, "…deaf to the siren songs of old metaphysical bird catchers who have been piping at him all too long, 'you are more, you are higher, you

---

[9] As stated in a note to the Preface, we will use "them" in this Essay to avoid gender specificity, which is not offered in the sermon itself, beyond the feminine declension natural to Syriac.
Not only parrot human-companions, but also scientists have a sense of how difficult it is to identify a parrot's gender. They are monomorphic, meaning that male and female parrots are indistinguishable to the eye. But they can tell each other apart, a sign of their parahuman abilities that exceed the human. Monomorphism has led artists and activists to take an interest in and to advocate for such nonhuman animals as a parallel phenomenon for ambiguous gender across species. Andy Warhol, for example, collaborated with the scientist Kurt Benirschke on an illustrated volume concerning endangered species, called *Vanishing Animals* (New York: Springer-Verlag, 1986); see 94–8 on the Puerto Rican Parrot. And see Anthony E. Grudin, *Like a Little Dog: Andy Warhol's Queer Ecologies* (Oakland: University of California Press, 2022), 99–118, on this project and its ramifications for understanding Warhol's complicated relationship with nonhuman animals.
The artists Jennifer Allora and Guillermo Calzadilla, in collaboration with the science-fiction writer Ted Chiang, made a haunting short film (*The Great Silence* from 2014) of a Puerto Rican parrot reflecting on the world's largest single aperture radio telescope, located in Esperanza, Puerto Rico. The telescope has been searching for sounds of life in the universe, but in a non-judgmental way, the parrot (speaking in subtitles) asks why humans don't listen more carefully to the languages (including the parrots') and sounds on Earth. The silent space above is not a replacement for the world of language right in front of us, the parrot states. See Michelle White, *Allora & Calzadilla: Specters of Noon* (Houston: Menil Collection, 2021), 42–3.
Parrots' monomorphism notwithstanding, the bird can also be a metaphor in medieval China for brides who surrender their liberty to their husbands, for example. They are "intelligence in chains," whose brilliant plumage (standing in for vanity) yet leads them to capture and sorrow. See Edward H. Schafer, *The Golden Peaches of Samarkand: A Study of T'ang Exotics* (Berkeley: University of California Press, 1963), 99–102, and also his "Parrots in Medieval China," in *Studia Serica Bernhard Karlgren Dedicata. Sinological Studies Dedicated to Bernhard Karlgren on his Seventieth Birthday October Fifth, 1959*, ed. Søren Egerod and Else Glahn (Copenhagen: Ejnar Munksgaard, 1959), 271–82, here 280. There is a long-standing connection between parrots and women across cultures; see Boria Sax, *Avian Illuminations: A Cultural History of Birds* (London: Reaktion, 2021), 137.

are of a different origin!'"[10] As he himself describes it, Isaac is not deaf to the parrot (the siren songs of old do not snare him), and he is no longer certain he is greater than, nor so different from, that small parrot.

Beginning with an extended interpretative summary of the sermon, focusing on the elements of *becoming* described and modelled by Isaac, this chapter also moves beyond the sermon to place Isaac's parrot within a long history of humanity's fascination with these birds. Parrots are "parabolic humanity," so thoroughly do they reveal us.[11] Their capacity for speech and mimicry has attracted us for our entire history. From ancient Greece to the Enlightenment, and within the development of western colonization, parrots have confounded human-other categories, as they have provided tropes by which animals can be seen to rise to the level of the human and (with our characteristic perversity) by which fellow humans could be relegated to the animal less-than-human. At the same time, the very otherness of the parrot lures. This chapter also examines transformative possibilities of becoming-other, particularly becoming-animal, possibilities that have been explored in contemporary animal studies and modern philosophy but have always existed as potential states of being.[12] Isaac finds ways to elevate his parrot to human and angelic status, though not without some ambivalence, and in the process folds his own voice and being (and his audience's) into parrot. It is that enfolding of subjects in Isaac's text that makes his text strikingly modern, even as it is deeply, ineluctably of its moment too. Isaac is a writer of remarkable agility and imagination, and we hope our approach to multiple facets of this sermon will reveal the extraordinary voices with which Isaac still addresses us.

Parrot religion is another topic opened by Isaac. How did this small bird, who cannot sin and therefore not know salvation as humans can,

---

[10] *Beyond Good and Evil: Prelude to a Philosophy of the Future*, ed. Rolf-Peter Horstmann and Judith Norman, trans. Judith Norman (Cambridge: Cambridge University Press, 2002), 123 [230].

[11] Hillel Schwartz, *The Culture of the Copy: Striking Likenesses, Unreasonable Facsimiles* (New York: Zone Books, 1996), 150, "Parrothood is a parabolic humanity."

[12] For example, see Melanie Challenger, *How to Be Animal: A New History of What It Means to Be Human* (New York: Penguin, 2021), *Animality/ Posthumanism/ Disability*, ed. Michael Lundblad, New Literary History, vol. 51, no. 4 (Baltimore: Johns Hopkins University, 2020), Bénédicte Boisseron, *Afro-Dog: Blackness and the Animal Question* (New York: Columbia University Press, 2018), Giovanni Aloi, *Speculative Taxidermy: Natural History, Animal Surfaces, and Art in the Anthropocene* (New York: Columbia University Press, 2018), and the important *Zoontologies: The Question of the Animal*, ed. Cary Wolfe (Minneapolis: University of Minnesota Press, 2003), as well as references below.

come to know God's will? And how did they come to follow that will more faithfully, more selflessly, than any humans did or could? As Serres writes above, sometimes it is only in religion that we can still hear and see our shared lives beyond our own species. And we can find animal religion, too. In Isaac's sermon, that is another mode of thinking, being, and writing in which parrots emerge as compelling creatures, almost equal to or as good as human (or sometimes even better than), a theme that runs throughout western history. Indeed, as some scientists argue that wolves taught us social life, some also place birds at the beginning of our ability to communicate through speech.[13] In other words, if speech and mind are the means by which religion emerges most fully (according to western tradition), we share traits with our creaturely companions on earth who also turn toward God.

Paraphrasing Isaac's Sermon: Parrot as Paradigm

This sermon is among the longest extant homiletic works in the Late Antique Syriac corpus. It surely asked a lot of its audience. It is driven by a narrative of encounter and transformation—of meeting a parrot, hearing its message, and adapting to its theological position fully. In that sense, it is a piece of storytelling meant to empower and captivate listeners: 'hear how this unexpected meeting changed everything for me and how it should change everything for you, too. Now we can *truly* know.' Moreover, it is an extended rumination on prophetic lineage and on the media of knowledge-transfer, which are not only human and animal, but also a wide variety of made things, including writing and musical instruments, crosses, and bridges, and so on. Speech circulates among all these objects, each part of a humming circuitry of divine revelation.

The sermon opens with a trumpeting of such media, "Your Cross is a speaking pen, for through it the silent have spoken" (l. 9). The cross and pen would normally be speechless, but God has endowed the former with the ability to speak and also to give speech to those things without that capacity normally. Sound is a consistent theme of the sermon: cross and pen, lyre and flute, and human sounds, intelligible (words, hymns) and otherwise (belches, howls). The oral is a frequent element evoked, such as the taste and feel of holy words in the mouth. And the parrot arrives early

---

[13] See Barbara Ballentine and Jeremy Hyman, *Bird Talk: An Exploration of Avian Communication* (Ithaca: Cornell University Press, 2021).

in the sermon, a foregrounding of the creature that firmly embeds these words and sounds. From the outset then, the parrot is the chirper, singer, or twitterer of faith (in Syriac, *l'ēz* [ܠܥܙ] 'singing,' 'chirping' or 'squawking'—the verb, as we'll see, used also for humans) for human hearing. For the parrot is a Sign of God (*remza d-Allaha* [ܪܡܙܐ ܕܐܠܗܐ]) that delivers wonder and knowledge, and they are a teacher of humans from a book of wisdom that is otherwise inaccessible. The parrot is furthermore a "skilled scribe," who made Isaac's tongue (which is speaking, singing, twittering the sermon) a pen for the riches delivered by the Cross for his audience (ll. 9–10).

In the opening section, the cross is a dominant motif. It brings speech to the otherwise speechless or unenlightened. But it is also imbricated in many features of the world, such as musical instruments, fire, springs, bridge, oven, tree, wall, tower, stairway, wing, gate, and key of life (ll. 41–72). The cross is widely and deeply embedded in human lives, in the made and natural features of human being and passage on earth. Indeed, it is a constituent part of creation.[14] And it continues to produce new callings and realities, which is what Isaac is left to unpack for his listeners and readers (ll. 73–4).

Isaac proceeds to describe his life-changing experience with the anonymous parrot—despite their crucial role, the parrot is left unnamed and undescribed, in any way that would let us identify them by species. Isaac claims God led him to this place, the great city of Antioch, in which Isaac had other adventures.[15] On this day, "a singular marvel encountered me" (l. 76). Before it entered his vision, it made itself heard, and he seems to have followed this voice sent by God to the great church of St. Peter. Turning a corner, or through a parting of the gathered crowd, one imagines, Isaac caught his glimpse of the source of this compelling sound, "that wise bird who was chirping the faith" (l. 82).[16] He joined the crowd and listened (one might recall: "Hear, O Israel. Ephphatha"). Opened, he thought hard, collected himself, and in amazement before this Sign, said

[14] See Peers, *Animism, Materiality and Museums*, 56.
[15] See the translation (RK) and analysis of Isaac and music in GP, *Byzantine Media Subjects* (Ithaca: Cornell University Press, 2024).
[16] Here might be a point to think of the city's soundscapes, places like the square before St. Peter's where particular kinds of voices and sonic interactions were possible. In that sense, the parrot is a soundmark within that active, contention-filled space. On soundscape and soundmark, Wendy Bellion, *Iconoclasm in New York: Revolution to Reenactment* (University Park: Pennsylvania State University Press, 2019), 59–106.

to himself, "this is a Sign of God, which has been stirred up through his providence" (l. 90). His wonderment is not inexplicable, because he recognizes that this wondrous speech from a bird in the market before the church was not a common way for the faith of the cross to be proclaimed (ll. 93–4). This was a particularly contentious moment for various Christian groups in the city, as we have seen, and Isaac calls attention to the heated conflicts among the groups. He is clear that there is a right and wrong side, between orthodox and the schismatics. However, he gives some indication that his own mind had not yet been made up, though he was clear when the parrot revealed to him which side was righteous in the eyes of the Lord (ll. 95–148).[17]

Isaac took a strong stance against the heresy of denying the Addition (explained above), which was the work of Satan and against all godly things, and he was able to do so because the voice of the parrot showed him so forcefully what the "hidden idol" was (l. 149). The bird chirped thrice (l. 150–1), and Isaac heard. He doesn't make this point overtly, but taking place before the church of Peter, some reference to Peter's betrayal of the Lord described in the Gospels would surely have entered his listeners' minds. But unlike the mighty apostle, Isaac did not betray the Lord at the bird's chirpings. The bird, as far as we can tell, spoke three times the refrain 'Holy, Holy God'. In this way, they chirped, played the lyre, sang a lullaby, all in true faith (ll. 150–6). The lullaby was for the child-like humans they were teaching, each according to their ability to discern (see l. 85). The bird was a wise teacher in their abilities measured to reach their students.

Isaac fell fully into his openness to the bird, and the following section is crucial for understanding the bridging of parrot and human subjects, and their mutual becoming. In this passage, Isaac repeats the parrot's refrain of 'Holy, Holy' in a rhythmic, repetitive chorus that lasts some 70 lines (ll. 157–226). In one way, Isaac is verbally riffing on the refrain, repeating the catchphrase, and following in these two-line sections with poetic evocations of the significance of the parrot's inspiration. And in another way, the writer is folding his voice into the parrot's, convinced by the truth of the bird's chirping, and now echoing the incantation through a hypnotic set of repetitions, in which the identity of speaker(s) loses clarity and

---

[17] See above for discussion of the theological background for Isaac's sermon, but see, also, De Giorgi and Eger, *Antioch: A History*, 198–200, where the parrot is mentioned, as is Peter the Fuller, but not Isaac himself.

definition.[18] And the parrot's own identity and magnitude increase in these entrancing reiterations. Isaac early states that the parrot's song and performance are angelic, paralleling the praise of the seraphim and watchers around the throne of God, and creating the nourishment angels need (ll. 158–61). He will also say later in the sermon that the outstretched wings of the parrot viscerally conflate angel and bird, while their voices likewise flow together in their compatible, indistinguishable songs of praise (see ll. 459–62).

This Sign of God fundamentally remade Isaac, and it made him parrot in all the ways an innocent creature (like angel and animal) can know and relate to God. Now parrot-like, Isaac could be more fully and truly Christian in his subject state. And he could lead his audience in honoring the Lord just as he learned from the parrot how to do. His changed state is poetically described at length: his mind trembled and exulted from what he drank. And Isaac came to see the parrot clearly in their majesty; the parrot is seated like a king with the crown of praises given to the bride of faith (ll. 243–8). Isaac can say the voice is not logical—it defies reason—but here the negotiation of animal-human difference enters, as it almost always does for us, although the voice is also a paradoxical Sign, just like the wine from water conjured by Jesus (ll. 253–4). The parrot was not deprived of words, Isaac says, and they were also sanctified words, that some inexplicably did not heed. Isaac took the Sign to heart, perhaps uniquely among those gathered there that day, and he left that crowd for prayer and contemplation in the church (ll. 259–64). His extended prayer is a meditation on the Christian economy under Isaac's reformed understanding of orthodoxy (ll. 265–344). His faith is newly made by the parrot, and Isaac is in that heightened state of new (almost dissociated) subjectivity, "for the bird's voice instructed me, that praised his majesty even more. For the mind had become drunk with the wonder and glory that it encountered, and he reclined with thanksgiving and was pleased with its delicacies" (ll. 342–4).

---

[18] See Tim Ingold, *The Perception of the Environment: Essays in Livelihood, Dwelling, and Skill* (New York: Routledge, 2000), 409, "We then realize that, far from deriving their meanings from their attachments to mental concepts, which are imposed upon a meaningless world of entities and events 'out there', *words gather their meanings from the relational properties of the world itself.* Every word has a compressed compacted history" [italics in original]. See, also, the important remarks on contact calls by Jean M. Langford, "Avian Bedlam: Toward a Biosemiosis of Troubled Parrots," *Environmental Humanities* 9, no. 1 (2017): 84–107.

The following section makes clear that Isaac's faith has been clarified and rejuvenated, "In the city, which I saw in a new way, I had seen something new with joy, a mouth that spoke in a new way, a new glory for the Son" (ll. 345–6). This small mouth, speaking from the tumult of the human crowd around it, broke through for Isaac; it created an original way to speak truth and brought fresh praise to God. Nothing was now the same for him, he says. The city was entirely new, and his senses were re-awoken to these words spoken by "a voice for the first time," which he drank "like an infant at the breast of his mother" (ll. 349–50). The fact that the bird had delivered these startling insights pushes Isaac to greater self-examination, to praise the Lord all the more fervently after witnessing the parrot's eloquence and wisdom. Reproved by the parrot, Isaac is clear he wants to be like the bird in their sincere and incisive understanding of God, "For the argument was not small for those discerning, if they seek it, since the bird with the words 'holy' proclaimed the faith" (ll. 383–4). Isaac is not certain how the bird came to their greater knowledge, either their own teaching or taught by their 'Sign' (ll. 387–92). And in any case, the bird is the most discerning of pupils, because they did not wonder or question, but accepted the answer (l. 394). Unlike students who need punishing and discipline to learn their lessons, the parrot accepted their instruction. The bird, astonishingly, learned without bruises (l. 414)! And they are the better student then, better than any human pupils, who have to apply themselves to arduous, patient learning. The parrot is truly an exemplary teacher: a new thing, Isaac proclaims, new in the ways it learns, sings, speaks, confesses, praises; they are a new harp and trumpet; and they are venerable like the seraphim and like the saints of the church (ll. 429–50).

Indeed, the parrot brings shame to Christians who had thought themselves righteous. Even a bird knows better. But the bird is already assimilated to godly realities. When they extend their wings, they are like the crucified one, "Let them be admonished by the bird who has administered the mysteries of the Cross, and by their words like a scribe teaches and offers admonition. Let them be ashamed by the spreading of [the parrot's] wings, which depict the mysteries of the cross, and by their gentle words, by which they recite the faith" (ll. 459–62). The apparently genderless parrot bridges human distinctions.[19] The bird in their body also, and not only in their voice, finds and declares union with God, "When they spread

---

[19] And see above on the difficulties of determining the sex of parrots, who are monomorphic.

out their wings, they depicted the beautiful image of the Cross, and when they opened their mouth, they chirped its faith and its truth" (ll. 465–6).

The parrot is not distracted by earthly things and shows their better righteousness these ways, too. Worldly power does not cow them, nor crowds of humans. The parrot is not tempted by money or jewels, nor are they frightened by threats of violence or weapons. Humble, they sing according to their own calling for the good of all around them (ll. 467–504). They are Christ-like in their unwavering adherence to the message of truth, undistracted and unbowed. But they are also, again, like the angels, particularly the seraphim, which they emulate and quote, "Holy, Holy, God, their tongue imitates and chirps, the verse that Isaiah wrote, by which the seraphim (cried) Holy" (ll. 507–8); and they are like the apostles, since they recite this revelatory verse from the Gospels (l. 510).

Isaac enters into a long series of admonitions at this point for his human listeners (ll. 511–94), and his lesson is clear: follow the example of the bird and be better humans and Christians. "Let not the sound of your harp cease from praise of the Crucified one" (l. 602)! The models of faith in the sacred past stand by Isaac's audience, and the parrot's and their examples will shore up their righteous convictions, even in the face of adversity. The litany of exemplars is the longest section of the sermon, this Cloud of Witness lasting almost 300 lines (ll. 637–928). Isaiah stands out as a particular model, an apt paradigm for the seraphic parrot, "Isaiah also raised his voice by what was praiseworthy among the prophets; faith taught him, 'Cry out at the top of your lungs'" (ll. 729–30). He spoke openly, like the parrot, but unlike Isaiah, the parrot also spans the angelic and prophetic, in voice and in body.

Addressed to a single disciple now (l. 929), the penultimate section of the sermon is an exhortation to take these lessons seriously and to follow that "band of the illustrious" (l. 931). In the final section, those lessons are summarized, and the audience is presented with good reason to try to outdo the parrot's faith. The adverb 'even' (ܐܦ – *'aph*) persuades Isaac's listeners: "for *even* the bird declared it" (l. 1010). And so should you, even more. The bird is in a deficit position in relation to the salvific potential of the human audience: it cannot take the eucharist, its species was not chosen for the Incarnation, it cannot be resurrected; but despite the promises not made to this bird, they were still diligent and forthright in their praises (ll. 1013–20). In these ways, the bird remains at the stage of fetus in relation to adult Christian listeners, "without sins and without reward" (l. 981). A Christian bird needs to have sinned in order to be redeemed, and they are halted at the developmental step before they can sin, a passage seemingly paused between revelation and redemption. Yet it is a venerable mode of revelation, for "the Spirit chirped through the Apostles" too (l. 1042), and Isaac enjoins his audience to be "a temple trumpet," "a living trumpet," to testify and chirp also (ll. 1043, 1047). The parrot is Isaac's glorious hero, "as for you, everything he had he gave to you, shout and proclaim his honors" (l. 1020). Like them, Isaac concludes, "be alert and chirp with me glory to the Father and to the Son and to the Holy Spirit" (l. 1068).

IMITATING PARROTS

Imitation runs through Isaac's sermon, from the parrot's repetition of the Addition to Isaac's repetition of the parrot, to the audience's own participation in this copying. "Be alert and sing with me." This chain of imitation mixes identities, human and animal, and they all become in Isaac's telling closer to God in this divine repetition. Imitation, resemblance, mimicry—in short, parroting—are fundamentally in play in Isaac's performance here, and such acts are the catalyst for the animal-becoming Isaac describes.

The tendency to imitation is a faceted trope in western thought, from Antiquity to the contemporary world. In Roman culture, the parrot could be a negative comparison for poets. Petronius, Ovid, and Statius adduced the parrot as the model for their disparaged competitors, who overly relied on past models for their compositions. However, those same poets also wrote sentimental poems about parrots, citing those very parrot voices, and they too drew on predecessors for various aspects of their verse.[20] Parrots operated as figures in other periods in western history to establish the proper relationship between originality of composition and reworking of past exemplars. But as in the Roman world, the judgment is not so straightforward.

While parrots copy, they simultaneously select, innovate, and remake what they have copied. For example, in the Stanley Kubrick film *The Killers* from 1956 (based on Lionel White's novel *Clean Break* from 1955), a parrot makes a crucial intervention that reveals the film's cynical moral: its

---

[20] Catherine M. Connors, *Petronius the Poet: Verse and Literary Tradition in the Satyricon* (Cambridge: Cambridge University Press, 1998), 47–9.

owners lying dead before them, the parrot states, "Not fair." Now, the parrot is repeating some of the humans' dying words, but it is also purposefully selecting the fragment that distills and unifies the entire narrative. Perhaps it is an incidental element in the narrative, but Kubrick purposefully inserted the bird moralist into the film; no parrot appears in the novel. The parrot clearly copies, but they also provide crucial retrospective meaning in their selective choice of speech. Of course, it's fiction (or a noir crime movie), but the bird stands for human interpretative agency in ways that only a parrot can. As Alan B. Bond and Judy Diamond write, "A parrot is not a tape recorder repeating the most common sounds it hears, but a cognitive agent making choices among alternative vocalizations that are expected to produce particular outcomes."[21] Kubrick's parrot, as Isaac's, is not a mechanical automaton. They are an agent with will; they can distill and perform an utterance; and they provide the perfect statement of conclusion and meaning of what had gone before.

There has always been some uncertainty over parrots' capacity for interpretative statements, however. In late medieval poetry, the nightingale and the parrot could be opposed as two contradictory modes of literary composition, the former composing ex novo, the latter derivatively. The latter's reliance on quotation over invention could be seen as a negative trait, but in practice, the two modes were not in opposition, because both drew on elements from past works and remade, elaborated, and devised new versions of them. As Sarah Kay argues, parrots quote, but they also enact a conscious play on recognition of their models, "which, by supposing anchorage in anterior subjects, enables subjective renewal and hence, potentially, subjective change."[22] In Late Antiquity, the cento genre, which was based on reworking classical texts, was highly popular, and it might be said, then, that the parrot is the literary totem of the period this

---

[21] Alan B. Bond and Judy Diamond, *Thinking Like a Parrot: Perspectives from the Wild* (Chicago: University of Chicago Press, 2019), 138.
[22] Sarah Kay, *Parrots and Nightingales: Troubadour Quotations and the Development of European Poetry* (Philadelphia: University of Pennsylvania Press, 2013), 23.

book is primarily focused on.[23] Exemplarity is a central concern and process of this period.

In Isaac's sermon, we might well ask who is mimicking whom. The parrot is quoting scripture, which is a transcription of prophetic witnessing of angelic speech, while they are also quoting the revised sanctus promulgated by Peter the Fuller. And Isaac in turn, and again and again, quotes the bird, in a kind of singsong even, that imitates a repetition and variation very common to birds (see ll. 149–226).[24] And he also falls into an abyss of citation this way, since by quoting the bird, and so repetitively, he is also in the chain of voices that is seraphim, Isaiah, parrot, and indeed every righteous Christian (and of course many others). This voiced imbrication

---

[23] See Kay, *Parrots and Nightingales*, 1, as well as, more broadly, Brian P. Sowers, "Herculean Centos: Myth, Polemics, and the Crucified Hero in Late Antiquity," in *Herakles Inside and Outside the Church: From the First Apologists to the End of the Quattrocento*, ed. Arlene L. Allan, Eva Anagnostou-Laoutides and Emma Stafford (Leiden: Brill, 2020), 94–115, Scott McGill, *Virgil Recomposed: The Mythological and Secular Centos in Antiquity* (Oxford: Oxford University Press, 2005), and M.D. Usher, *Homeric Stitchings: The Homeric Centos of the Empress Eudocia* (Lanham, MD: Rowman & Littlefield, 1998).

[24] See Mark Payne, "The Understanding Ear: Synaesthesia, Paraesthesia and Talking Animals," in *Synaesthesia and the Ancient Senses*, ed. Shane Butler and Alex Purves (Durham: Acumen, 2013), 43–52, here 47, quoting Aristotle, *Parts of Animals*, 2.17, 660a35-b3, "All birds make use of their tongue to communicate with one another and some very much more so than others, so that with some there does indeed seem to be an exchange of knowledge among them."

See this examination of the nightingale musicality by a musician: David Rothenberg, *Nightingales in Berlin: Searching for the Perfect Sound* (Chicago: University of Chicago Press, 2019), for example, 48, "Music is an exercise in contrast between the expected and the unexpected, the beat and the stop, the patterned and the patternless." The interspecies connections and echoes are drawn out vividly in his writing and in his playing, for a recording also called *Nightingales in Berlin* that was released in 2019 (https://www.nightingalesinberlin.com/2019/1/23/lbmgp1qg9ytg6muidaoar1m0utv2wm).

See Ani Patel, John Iversen, Micah Bregman, and Irena Schulz, "Experimental Evidence for Synchronization to a Musical Beat in a Nonhuman Animal," *Current Biology* 19, no. 10 (2009): 827–30, who argue that a white parrot named Snowball could follow a beat, a trait not believed to be possible among nonhuman animals. The neural circuitry necessary for open-ended vocal learning and the ability to imitate nonverbal movements are rare traits, according to these scientists, only found in parrots and humans.

In a related mode, see Nina Amstutz, "The Avian Sense for Beauty: A Posthumanist Perspective on the Bowerbird," *Art History* 44, no. 5 (2021): 1038–64, on using "the bowerbird's ornamental displays as a point of departure to rethink how historians have circumscribed human creative activity, which has been defined in opposition to the animal by our institutions of art since at least the eighteenth century," and on "how animals act as creative subjects independent of their interactions with humans."

of subjects is deeply embedded in Christian senses of self and its relations to sacred history and, indeed, to God. The most well-known example of enfolded voices across time and text is Athanasius of Alexandria on the Psalms' layered identities of God, David, and every subsequent reader/reciter.[25]

These biases to mimicry are, in any case, simply built-in. That view goes back at least as far as Aristotle.[26] But Walter Benjamin also famously wrote, "Nature creates similarities. One need only think of mimicry. The highest capacity for producing similarities, however, is man's. His gift of seeing resemblances is nothing other than a rudiment of the powerful

---

[25] *The Life of Antony and The Letter to Marcellinus*, trans. R. C. Gregg (New York: Paulist Press, 1985), 107–8, with emendations from http://www.athanasius.com/psalms/aletterm.htm, "With this book, however, though one does read the prophecies about the Saviour in that way, with reverence and with awe, in the case of all the other Psalms, it is as though it were one's own words that one read; and anyone who hears them is moved at heart, as though they voiced for him his deepest thoughts…Not as the words of the patriarchs or of Moses and the other prophets will he reverence these: no, he is bold to take them as his own and written for his very self. Whether he has kept the Law or whether he has broken it, it is his own doings that the Psalms describe; everyone is bound to find his very self in them and, be he faithful soul or be he sinner, each reads in them descriptions of himself. It seems to me, moreover, that because the Psalms thus serve him who sings them as a mirror, wherein he sees himself and his own soul, he cannot help but render them in such a manner that their words go home with equal force to those who hear him sing and stir them also to a like reaction."

[26] See Rebecca Bushnell, *The Marvels of the World: An Anthology of Nature Writing Before 1700* (Philadelphia: University of Pennsylvania Press, 2021), 3, "Complementing this belief in the material interaction between humans and their environment, the premodern habit of mind saw all that is human reflected in the nonhuman world in a vast network of correspondences and resemblances…This idea that a human being is thus a microcosm had the power to deconstruct the human into those constituent analogies with other creatures and matter. As much as theologians and philosophers asserted human exceptionalism and supremacy over all other living things, both in their bodies and in the book of nature, people were all too like those other beings."

compulsion in former times to become and behave like something else."[27] In this view, we ourselves are natural, obsessive mimics. Sharing voice, movement, being across species, that's just what we do and participate in, however much we downplay or ignore it. Isaac, parrot, and audience through his text are just performing a natural chain of resemblance and mutual making.

Perhaps one more example, this time from Byzantine romance, will demonstrate the common spread of these resemblances and formations across species. In the novel *Livistros and Rodamni*, a remarkable encounter takes place among the eponymous characters and a parrot.[28] Rodamni appears to the hero in sumptuous dress ("Over a red and gold garment, she wore a brightly colored cloak that trailed far back over the ground") and with a loquacious companion. As Livistros describes her, "In one hand, she held a tame parrot, who sat there without constraint and said in a human voice, 'This lady makes slaves of souls not yet possessed by passion, and she shackles hearts still free; she subdues the senses of those reared in the mountains and desolate places.' And I paused from gazing at that wondrous lady with her rare beauty and indescribable appearance,

---

[27] Walter Benjamin, "On the Mimetic Faculty," in *Reflections: Essays, Aphorisms, Autobiographical Writing*, ed. Peter Demetz, trans. Edmund Jephcott (New York: Harcourt, 1978), 333–6, here 333 [= "Über das mimetische Vermögen," in *Sprache und Geschichte: Philosophische Essays*, ed. Rolf Tiedemann (Stuttgart: Reclam, 1992), 91–4, here 91].

And see Christopher GoGwilt, "Of Mimicry, Birds, and Words: The Technology of Starling Song in European, American, and Indonesian Poetry," in *Mocking Bird Technologies: The Poetics of Parroting, Mimicry and Other Starling Tropes*, ed. Christopher GoGwilt and Melanie D. Holm (New York: Fordham University Press, 2018), 213–37, Dorit Bar-On, "Communicative Intentions, Expressive Communication, Origins of Meaning," in *The Routledge Handbook of Philosophy of Animal Minds*, ed. Kristin Andrews and Jacob Beck (Abingdon: Routledge, 2017), 301–12, Jennifer Ackerman, *The Bird Way: A New Look at How Birds Talk, Work, Play, Parent, and Think* (New York: Penguin, 2020), 65–86, as well as Michael T. Taussig, *Mimesis and Alterity: A Particular History of the Senses* (London: Routledge, 1993).

[28] See *Three Medieval Greek Romances: Velthandros and Chrysandza, Kallimachos and Chrysorroi, Livistros and Rodamni*, trans. Gavin Betts (New York: Routledge, 1995), 95–192, here 141 (slightly emended).

The conceit of the parrot is applied also in the imaginative literary evocation by Panagiotis A. Agapitos, "The Bookseller's Parrot: A Fictional Afterword," in *Reading the Late Byzantine Romance: A Handbook*, ed. Adam J. Goldwyn and Ingela Nilsson (Cambridge: Cambridge University Press, 2019), 321–39, here 327–31 ('Second Part, in Which an Italian Student Talks about Travelling Tales and a Clever Bird Is Discovered to Be a Literary Figure'). Agapitos calls his fictional parrot Livistros.

and marveled at how the bird had been enslaved and was able to tell of their servitude with human voice." No other word is spoken, but the parrot's; the humans are mute. And the parrot grabs attention with their claim that the woman is an enslaver of souls and senses, human and nothuman; they are able to describe it clearly and forcefully, and thus Livistros's wonderment at their speech *and* self-awareness. His wonderment stifles his language, however, and it makes a parrot out of him: "It was dawn when I saw the lady crossing the meadow. I came out of my tent, and in my joy, I set out. I really seemed to be going on clouds. All rough ground is level in the path of a man whose soul is dreaming of a lady's love. My friend, I seemed to have wings. Quickly, in the very twinkling of an eyelid, I reached the spot that the lady's eunuch had indicated to me." Not only was Livistros captured by the gorgeous woman, but he was also subsumed to parrot-state in his obedient bird-like transformation. He can now fly, he can travel quickly like a bird, he can range among the clouds, but he cannot yet speak. Then the lady tells him to speak, and he finds words for her. He has been parroted by love—captured, tamed, transformed.

Knowing Parrots

Isaac was then not alone in traversing species boundaries between human and parrot. The abilities of parrots, and other birds, to speak and convince auditors of their subject states, or at least shake their certainties of human linguistic priority, go back to Antiquity and extend through almost all of western history.[29] The ways in which speaking birds figure in ancient

---

[29] The best sources on the histories and meanings of the parrot are Bruce T. Boehrer, *Parrot Culture: Our 2500-Year-Long Fascination with the World's Most Talkative Bird* (Philadelphia: University of Pennsylvania Press, 2004), and Paul Carter, *Parrot* (London: Reaktion, 2006). Excellent recent studies of animal language in this period include *Animal Languages in the Middle Ages: Representations of Interspecies Communication*, ed. Alison Langdon (New York: Palgrave Macmillan, 2018), and Jonathan Hsy, "Between Species: Animal-Human Bilingualism and Medieval Texts," in *"Booldly bot meekly": Essays on the Theory and Practice of Translation in the Middle Ages in Honor of Roger Ellis*, ed. Catherine Batt and René Tixier (Turnhout: Peeters, 2018), 563–79.

writers largely fall to their exceptional qualities, namely speech, and those writers were often vague about the particular species they were describing.[30]

Speaking, winged agents are not uncommon in the history of western culture, as we'll see. Writing about his time in the Persian court in the late fifth century B.C.E., the Greek doctor Ctesias described a memorable encounter with a new species,

> There is a bird called the *bittakos* that has a human voice, is capable of speech, and grows to the size of a falcon. It has a crimson face and a black beard and is dark blue as far as the neck…like cinnabar. It can converse like a human in Indian but if taught Greek, it can also speak Greek.[31]

He is clear that the bird had speech, and it had linguistic range—a language is never natural, but always acquired through study and thought. The bird in these ways entered the realm of the civilized, for Ctesias is clear that it converses like a human, but in Greek also, and so it transcends barbarian, the other-human category, and joins the blessed Hellenes in conversing in a civilized tongue. Aelian also says that, in India, parrots are sacred birds among Brahmins, because of their speech.

> There too parrots are kept and crowd around the king. But no Indian eats a parrot in spite of their great numbers, the reason being that the Brahmins regard them as sacred and even place them above all other birds. And they add that they are justified in so doing, for the parrot is the only bird that gives the most convincing imitation of human speech. (*NA* 13.18)

Such birds also have power of discernment and self-control. Plutarch tells the story of a jay who was silenced by the trumpets at a funeral for a time, but that state was their choice, for it was:

---

[30] See, for an excellent analysis, Ashleigh Green, *Birds in Roman Life and Myth* (London: Routledge, 2023), 179–86.

The lack of precision of species and gender is a typical evasion of parrots' challenging polymorphism. See the remarks in Carter, *Parrot*, 8.

[31] Andrew G. Nichols, *Ctesias: On India. Translation and Commentary* (London: Bloomsbury, 2011), 47. He conjectures the bird was a plum-headed parakeet. And see *The Culture of Animals in Antiquity: A Sourcebook with Commentaries*, ed. Sian Lewis and Lloyd Llewellyn-Jones (Abingdon: Routledge, 2018), 268–72, J.M. Bigwood, "Ctesias' Parrot," *Classical Quarterly* 43, no. 1 (1993): 321–7, and Deborah Levine Gera, "Viragos, Eunuchs, Dogheads, and Parrots in Ctesias," in *Greeks between East and West: Essays in Greek Literature and History in Memory of David Asheri*, ed. Gabriel Herman and Israel Shatzman (Jerusalem: Israel Academy of Science and Humanities, 2007), 75–92, here 89–91 on parrots.

…an inner discipline and withholding of its mimetic skill, while it adjusted and refashioned its voice like a musical instrument. For suddenly its voice returned, and in place of its old repertoire of imitations rang out the music of the trumpets, reproducing all its sequences and every variation in melody and rhythm.[32]

The bird was capable of admirable re-tooling of their repertoire, after careful consideration.

That compelling—if always elusive—mixture of voice and speech, mind, and will, emerges in a range of recognition stories about birds in the ancient and medieval worlds.[33] There are several versions of stories of birds who greeted Augustus, and in recognition of their intelligence, the great Roman ended up purchasing them with unsuppressed pleasure.[34] Several versions also circulated about the Carthaginian Hanno, who had birds that could testify to his divine nature by saying, "Hanno is god." In one version, according to Aelian, "[freed] they sang their natural songs and made their bird music, saying a loud goodbye to Hanno and the lessons learned in their forced captivity," while in another story, the released birds were able to speak their mind (after being turned by Hanno's enemies) and could subvert Hanno's claims, "He shut us up and forced us to say he was a god."[35]

Moreover, parrots appear in medieval sources, both Latin and Greek, to recognize and confirm the claims of popes and emperors to their offices. The first mention in a papal court was during the reign of Leo IX (1049–54), who had a parrot who could speak his name and, like Augustus before him,

---

[32] *Moralia* 973c-e, trans. Jeremy Wynott, *Birdscapes, Birds in the Ancient World: Winged Words* (Oxford: Oxford University Press, 2018), 143.

[33] See now Bligh [Bethany] Somma, "'What the Swallow Describes and the Hoopoe Reports': The Iḫwān al-ṣafā᾿ and the Riddle of a Shared World," *Falsafa: Jahrbuch für islamische Religionsphilosophie* 4 (2022): 97–117, as well as their forthcoming "The Brethren of Purity on Justice for Animals and the Moral Demands of Rational Hierarchy," *Journal of the History of Philosophy*, and Peter Adamson and Bligh Somma, "Faḫr al-Dīn al-Rāzī on Animal Cognition and Immortality," *Archiv für Geschichte der Philosophie* (2021): 1–30.

[34] See Macrobius, *Saturnalia*, ed. and trans. Robert A. Kaster, 3 vols. (Cambridge, MA: Harvard University Press, 2011), I: 358 (II.29–30), on the parrot (*psittacus*), and the passage mentions a raven (*corvus*) and a magpie (*pica*), both of whom praise Augustus also.

[35] *Miscellany* XIV 30; trans. Wynott, *Birdscapes*, 148. See also Catherine Osborne, *Rethinking Early Greek Philosophy: Hippolytus of Rome and Presocratics* (Ithaca: Cornell University Press, 1987), 71–2, 232–3.

became greatly attached to them.[36] And earlier, during the reign of Basil I (867–86), a parrot predicted the coming reign of Leo VI (886–912), which was not self-evident at all times before his father's death, but the parrot acclaimed Leo in advance, "ai, ai, Kyrie Leon."[37] The parrot's life after their correct prediction is unfortunately not recorded. That momentary, if crucial, appearance on stage characterizes most such mentions, and it marks the exploitative assumptions about birds in literary narrative.

Parrots and other birds had a deeply rooted reputation for knowing things and events humans didn't.[38] Michel Serres wrote movingly about the addiction to birds that was the basis of ancient augury. He claimed the Romans were so successful because they paid little attention to language but watched the flight of birds, the peckings of chickens—those were the experts to observe.[39] Knowing birds comes from political choice. As Serres wrote,

> Without being able to prove it I believe, like soothsayers and haruspices, and like scientists, that there exists a world independent of men…I believe, I know, I cannot demonstrate the existence of this world without us. Who would rather not take dictation from its formidable silence, joyously and in good health, than write under the judgement of some tribunal?

Birds in this politics are active, necessary constituents, "active players in knowing worlds rather than passive bearers of features available to

---

[36] See Agostino Paravicini Bagliani, "Il pappagallo del papa: 'volatile parlante' e specchio di sovranità," in *Animali parlanti: Letteratura, teatro, canzoni*, ed. Caterina Mordeglia, Micrologus Library, vol. 82 (Florence: Galluzzo, 2017), 69–84, as well as Boehrer, *Parrot Culture*, 23–4.

[37] *Theophanes Continuatus, Iohannes Cameniata, Symeon Magister, Georgius Monachus*, ed. I. Bekker (Bonn: Weber, 1838), 698AB [21].

[38] Carter, *Parrot*, 67–75, and Boehrer, *Parrot Culture*, 33. This ability is well-attested in times of natural disaster, like earthquake. See Eugene Linden, *The Parrot's Lament: And Other True Tales of Animal Intrigue, Intelligence and Ingenuity* (New York: Dutton, 1999), 165–6.

[39] Michel Serres, *The Five Senses: A Philosophy of Mingled Bodies (I)*, trans. Margaret Sankey and Peter Cowley (London: Bloomsbury, 2016), 99–103. And see Catherine Michael Chin, "After Post, or, Animal Religion in an Age of Extinction," *Ancient Jew Review* (29 May 2018).

On birds like ostriches used in public games and vultures for sacrifice, see Jacopo De Grossi Mazzorin and Claudia Minniti, "The Exploitation and Mobility of Exotic Animals: Zooarchaeological Evidence from Rome," in *The Role of Zooarchaeology in the Study of the Western Roman Empire*, ed. Martyn G. Allen, Journal of Roman Archaeology Supplement, vol. 107 (Portsmouth, R.I.: Journal of Roman Archaeology, 2019), 85–99, here 91, and also Henriette Kroll, "Animals in the Byzantine Empire: An Overview of the Archaeozoological Evidence," *Archeologia Medievale* 39 (2012): 93–121, here 101–2 on domestic poultry and 102–5 on winged game.

knowledge."[40] Speech didn't always have to come into it. But birds can listen in and know: Ecclessiastes 10:20 evokes the enigmatic engagement with our words and their meanings that birds hear and report. Be careful what you say, even in private, for "a bird of the air shall carry the voice, and that which hath wings shall tell the matter" (KJV).[41]

Birds' abilities to know, to listen, to learn, as well as to report and to speak, have always made them uncanny fellow creatures. For Serres, our own speech and rationality arise from these very acts of bird participation and knowledge. Just as some biologists theorize our language descends from bird song, so birds deliver its meanings and possibilities. Birds as prophets are just one special category of these knowing animals, and Isaac clearly saw his parrot as prophetic in the venerable lineage of Isaiah, among others.

These events from antiquity are parrots' only appearances in the historical record, always for their capacity to match human speech and outdo human knowledge. How these situations come about is a matter for discussion: we're dealing with worlds of text, highly self-interested reports of possible events.[42] But their consistency is striking, they have good pedigree with stories from the past, and they do accord with most modern experience too, since we also still find parrots' speech so distinctive, remarkable, and often surprising. Missing in these accounts is a recognition of the deeply relational ways of interacting and learning that birds like parrots fold into.[43]

---

[40] Steve Hinchliffe, "Sensory Biopolitics: Knowing Birds and a Politics of Life," in *Humans, Animals and Biopolitics: The More-Than-Human Condition*, ed. Kristin Asdal, Tone Druglitrø, and Steve Hinchliffe (London: Routledge, 2017), 152.

[41] In the way that animals, women, and slaves have been consigned in the past to categories of less-than-human, World War II propaganda also warned soldiers (especially officers) against speaking too openly before women, with slogans like, "Keep mum, she's not so dumb. Careless talk costs lives."

[42] J.M. Coetzee, *The Lives of Animals* (Princeton: Princeton University Press, 1999), 51, "Thus the poem is not a gift to its object, as the love poem is. It falls within an entirely human economy in which the animal has no share."

[43] See Meredith J. West and Andrew P. King, "Mozart's Starling," *American Scientist* 78 (1990): 106–14, here 113, "An analogy with the capacities of echo-locating animals may be appropriate. Like bats or dolphins emitting sounds to estimate distance, some birds may bounce sounds off the animate environment, using behavioral reverberations to gauge the effects of their vocal efforts. They are not using Thorpe's behavioral mirror, necessary for self-reflection, but instead a social sounding board with which to shape functional repertoires."

Or Hinchliffe, "Sensory Biopolitics", 158, "Humans are predicated in nonhumans."

Such stories must have culturally conditioned Isaac's attitudes about parrots' power of discernment on some level, because they were not at all uncommon—they run as a thread through western culture of the last two and a half millennia. Isaac witnessed a parrot speaking true theology in a square before a church in Antioch; that is the assumption behind our treatment here. But Isaac does not have to have seen this bird at that moment for his story to be 'true'.[44] He may well have manipulated a story about a parrot in order to make a compelling and unusual sermon to bring his audience over to his side doctrinally—perhaps he is imitating and altering the Hanno story, like a parrot would do? Isaac is a Late Antique writer, deeply invested in exemplarity, and adapting a deserving model is not only what a good writer of the period was expected to do, but it was also very much a parrot-like behavior. The parrot did all the literary work Isaac needed them to do, and they still provided catalyst for the remaking of Isaac's human subject position vis-à-vis animal and God. Isaac didn't need to see a parrot, but he still needed a parrot because parrots fulfilled essential narrative functions for human self-knowing of free will, mind, speech, and relation to God.

Parrots and Their Religion

Isaac gave his parrot true Christian faith. According to the text, the parrot has sincere, authentic, and miraculous command of correct doctrine (ll. 147–76, 227–60). On one level, this understanding serves Isaac's positions perfectly well, since he wants to get across his didactic point with clarity and verve, and the parrot allows this delivery effectively to happen. On another level, Isaac disrupts expectations by imbuing the parrot with piety, that is, a desire to perform a ritual formula that joins them to humans

[44] See the helpful methodological reflections in A.J. Smith and B. Garlick, "'A green Parrot for a good Speaker': Writing with a Birds-Eye View in Eliza Haywood's *The Parrot*," in *Animal Satire*, ed. Robert McKay and Susan McHugh (Cham: Palgrave Macmillan, 2023), 140–1, "Unlike these mimicking antecedents, Haywood's parrot is rather an editorial agent who intentionally and discriminately curates information, reconfiguring the world of the reader in a way that this essay recognises as the process of writing *through* the animal. Such a process names a speculative practice of commenting upon the foibles and limitations of human society by seeking to inhabit the external vantage point, and alternative social existence, afforded to the nonhuman. Consequently, writing through the animal proves an effective satirical technique to both make strange the familiar relations of human existence and to illuminate the other, parallel, yet interwoven forms of living that co-constitute and unfold through such relations."

on earth and angels in heaven; according to Isaac, they have true faith and practice it. They are diminished by their lack of sin, which denies them salvation, a quality that only intensifies their angelic status. They are fetal or infant to our adult state, Isaac states, but without the capacity to grow into sin and thus gain salvation (l. 350). And yet Isaac wants some of that parrot grace for himself and his audience, and he works to find ways to move into that state, however partially and temporarily.

With religion granted by Isaac, the parrot comes closer to human than almost all animals, since religion is often said to be the exclusive preserve of the human.[45] Religion, indeed, is the least animal part of the human, it has been said and also assumed. Reason and language, or logos, are the *sine qua non* of religion, at least from a Christian-centered perspective.[46] Being able to make the distinction between human and animals has also been an important characteristic for understanding other humans' religion; too close an identification with animal means human discretion and superiority are broken, and that version of religion, proximate to animals', has been relegated to the primitive stage (or perhaps fetal stage) of human civilization.[47] (We'll return to this question with the Amazonian Bororó, below.) We're better able to entertain this possibility now and to grant religion to animals, but these positions are only now emerging.

Attributing religion to parrots is not unique to Isaac. In the range of periods and cultures in which textual testimony is found about parrots learning and controlling religious forms, that capacity to acquire religion

---

[45] See Paul Robert Matthews, "Why Animals and Religion Now?" *Humanimalia* 9, no. 1 (2018): 68–91, and Paul Christopher Johnson, *Automatic Religion: Nearhuman Agents of Brazil and France* (Chicago: University of Chicago Press, 2021).

[46] And yet animals undermine our claims to an exclusive relationship to the category of religion. See, for example, Donovan O. Schaefer, *Religious Affects: Animality, Evolution, and Power* (Durham, NC: Duke University Press, 2015).

[47] See Jennifer L. Koosed, "Moses: The Face of Fear," *Biblical Interpretation* 22 (2014): 428–9, "The history of religion can also be read as a history of trying to escape from the animal. The hierarchies of religion as constructed by the histories of religion place animal-centered religions at the bottom and human-centered religions, especially the most androcentric tradition (Christianity where God and man merge), at the top. But there is no escape from the animal—not in philosophy, not in religion, and not in life. Moses is the giver of the Law, the one who forges the people of Israel into a nation: a nation under its one, unimaginable God, for the first law commands monotheism and the second forbids images. And yet, the animal slides and sticks and claws. The image of Moses glowing/Moses horned evokes the very idolatry it seeks to repress. The animal reemerges and is transformed…Moses descends the mountain as Father, Law, and Animal, glorified, horned. Moses inhabits the spaces in between."

is deeply, inextricably parrot—and therefore animal and human both.[48] In the fourteenth-century Persian text, the *Ṭūṭī-Nāma* (*Tales of a Parrot*), for example, a parrot (tautologically) called Tuti performs a kind of *1001 Nights* litany of storytelling in order to forestall its demise, and he also makes strong claims to be a devout and learned Muslim,

> Though I may be a handful of feathers, because of the extent of my knowledge, I triumph over all. Theologians are amazed at my eloquence, and men of great wisdom are astonished at my ability in debating. I am not a messenger of God, though I am wearing green. I am not a houri with a cloak over my shoulder. I am not a zealot, but I can travel as a devout servant of God. I am religious, but I have wings. I am not a king, but I am worthy of a high position. I am not a scribe, but I am eloquent. 'Praise be to God: I am an excellent speaker.'[49]

The bird has a very sure sense of their religious abilities and convictions, including wisdom, discernment, and knowledge.[50] Perhaps Isaac's parrot had a similar sense of confidence; certainly, they proclaim the truth in the profession of the Addition. They had wings, but they also proclaimed true religion for Isaac.

---

[48] See Schwartz, *The Culture of the Copy*, 143–73.

[49] Ziya'u'd-din Nakhshabi, *Tales of a Parrot: The Cleveland Museum of Art's Ṭūṭī-Nāma*, ed. and trans. Muhammad A. Simsar (Cleveland: The Cleveland Museum of Art-Graz: Akademische Druck u. Verlagsanstalt, 1978), 8.

See also Italo Calvino, "Introduction," in *Italian Folktales*, trans. George Martin (New York: Harcourt Brace Jovanovich, 1980), who declares the parrot the symbol of storytelling, but the figure also stands for the freedom of the storyteller. The storyteller parrot is the commoner who creates. See xxxi, "It is a symbolic defense of the narrative art against those who accuse it of being profane and hedonistic. The suspense of the story keeps the fascinated listener from transgression." And the story *The Parrot* has the eponymous creature sustaining narrative indefinitely, so the king cannot reach a girl distracted by the stories; in the end, the parrot reveals himself a king in disguise, a handsome youth, who marries the girl himself (45–8). Moreover, in another story, the king only *listens*: see Adriana Cavarero, *For More Than One Voice: Toward a Philosophy of Vocal Expression*, trans. Paul A. Kottman (Stanford: Stanford University Press, 2005), 1–7.

[50] And see *Divine Stories: Divyavadana. Part I*, trans. Andy Rotman (Boston: Wisdom Publications, 2008), 333–6, 'The Story of the Two Parrot Chicks' (16): both chicks, having been instructed, incited, inspired, and delighted by the Blessed One's discourse on the Dharma, were then eaten by a cat, though reborn among the gods of Four Groups of the Great Kings.

In the western Christian tradition, stories of religious parrots are also widely attested. For example, a medieval Occitan poem described a devout bird who, when threatened with death, converts, but remains a true Christian, never failing to invoke God, and revealing itself to be anxious for the presence of the church and respectful of its sacraments.[51] An African Gray parrot at the Vatican was able to recite the Apostle's Creed, and a number of Early Modern poems describe parrots and other birds praising the Lord.[52] And in eighteenth-century France, a poem about a parrot called Ver-Vert described how pious such a parrot could be, but also how they could be led astray, proof of the dangers of simple recitation and mimicry, but in another way so very human in their capacity for sin.[53] Here is the negative (if also richly faceted) example of religious animals, which only expands the range of possibilities for religious discernment among such creatures, very similarly ranging to human possibilities, in fact. These examples are mere samples from a wide tradition of parrots practicing religion, very well and not so well, according to their discernment and abilities, but that is the point; the same could be said of humans.

Parrot Pupils

How did those sacred and true words reach the parrot? How did the bird get religion? It remained a mystery for Isaac, though he speculated on the questions (ll. 383–420). Were they taught, did it come to them through

---

[51] Suzanne Thiolier-Méjean, "Le motif du perroquet dans deux Nouvelles d'oc," in *Miscellanea mediaevalia: Mélanges offerts à Philippe Ménard*, ed. J. Claude Faucon, Alain Labbé, and Danielle Quéruel, 2 vols. (Paris: Champion, 1998), II: 1364–5.

[52] See *Two Early Renaissance Bird Poems: The Harmony of Birds, The Parliament of Birds*, ed. Andrew Malcolm (Washington, D.C.: Folger Shakespeare Library, 1984), 46, 60.

[53] See Louise E. Robbins, *Elephant Slaves and Pampered Parrots: Exotic Animals in Eighteenth-Century Paris* (Baltimore: Johns Hopkins University Press, 2002), 148; John Gilmore, "The Nunnery Parrot: Gresset's *Ver-Vert* and his English Translators," in *The Role of the Parrots in Selected Texts from Ovid to Jean Rhys: Telling a Story from an Alternative Viewpoint*, ed. Julia Courtney and Paula James (Lewiston: Edwin Mellen Press, 2006), 59–85; and Jean-François Counillon, "Le XVIIIe siècle de J.-B. Gresset et 'Ver-Vert'," *Bulletin de la Société d'émulation du bourbonnais* 67 (1995): 380, "un perroquet dévot, Une belle âme innocemment guidée; Jamais du mal n'avait eu l'idée, Ne disant onc un immodeste mot; Mais en revanche, il savait des cantiques, Des *oremus*, des colloques mystiques; Il disait bien son *benedicite*, Et *notre mère*, et *votre charité*, Il savait même un peu de soliloque, Et des traits fins de Marie Alacoque," and after his journey, he became the wrong kind of echo, 381, "Il entonna tous les horribles mots Qu'il avait au rapporter des bateaux…Les jeunes soeurs crurent qu'il parlait grec."

some insight of their own, or was it an inspiration from above? In any case, the Sign was not minor, and it was delivered as a reminder and rebuke, and as a model. Those considerations were crucial for human understanding of the meaning of the revelation. Human correction was dependent on acceptance of an animal version of Christianity, not on uncovering the precise origin and mechanism of it. The power of the Lord's mercy is revealed this way (l. 390). The bird did not wonder, so why should even an eloquent human dispute it?

The best human students need persuasion and coercion to reach the right answers and proper knowledge. But the parrot needed none of this. The parrot was a perfect, perhaps unique student (see ll. 427–30), not requiring punishment or rewards for their wondrous performance—no need for bruising, slapping, terrorizing, Isaac points out. Insights into fifth-century pedagogy can be gleaned from a lengthy passage in which Isaac makes his point about the relative ease of the bird's pliability and discernment,

> Until a teacher is mightily moved and puts on fury and threats, and through fear and terror places examples in the soul. A tutor presses him and raises the rod for his discipline, and then opens the sense of his intellect to receive teaching. He slaps his cheeks threateningly and tears out the locks of his hair, and then his mind becomes flexible, in order to speak the inflection of (his) words. He offers his back to the pillar (for scourging), as well as his side to the whips, and then he understands how to determine the knowledge of their concepts. His body is full with bruises, and swellings rise up on him, and then he becomes malleable to receive the aphorisms in their differences. He grabs his neck and drags him, and pulls the ears of the youth, and then he becomes malleable to discern the principles and inner treasures of knowledge. He brings him as if to a furnace and pours discipline into him, and then being obedient he pours a seal of learning upon his mind. Through suffering and torments, he refines and chastens him with abuses, and then (the student) adopts the image in himself of knowledge and of meaning. If a human being in this way becomes malleable toward learning; how did the bird without bruises learn the composition? (ll. 397–414)

Isaac's description of how children learned is far from current standards of pedagogy, but it is unlikely to be far from the actual situation he knew. Corporal punishment in the classroom is well attested in the education of children in the Roman world, and so is it also in relation to teaching parrots, in fact. Both Pliny and Apuleius describe the necessity of beating parrots for getting them to learn. Pliny says that the parrot has a particular hardness of beak and head, so that "when it is being taught to speak it is beaten on the head with an iron rod—otherwise, it does not feel blows" (*NH* X.58.117) and will not learn. For Pliny, parrots are also prone to drunkenness, which also (he claimed) aids their acquisition of language. This deficient version of parrots, as near-human but much less, is also found in Apuleius, who recommends tough learning for parrots, which possess only an inferior version of human speech and a mere mimicry, in any case.[54] However, pedagogy in the Roman world was not in the first place predicated on teaching critical and inventive thinking, but rather directed toward the acquisition of fundamental texts and precepts through repetition and memorization. Pedagogy was already parrot-like.

This description of pedagogy in the sermon then plays with easy assumptions of how parrots, for one, acquire speech and what they do with it. Hanno's birds learned to say what they needed to for him to feel he could release them, but then they disregarded their brief and even found ways actively to subvert his desire to have his divinity announced by such impeccable messengers. And Mozart's famous starling had a role in his composition, it seems; Mozart was not himself solely responsible for his music, which was sometimes animal-aided.[55] Alexander Humboldt reported having heard an Amazonian parrot speak a language only they spoke, since the humans who had once spoken it with them had been exterminated; the language then died with the parrot, it seems, before they could teach it and create new sociality.[56] Moreover, anyone who has lived with a parrot knows well who controls the conversation; the response is almost always the human reflexively returning the bird's words or

---

[54] See Latarzyna Kleczkowska, "Those Who Cannot Speak: Animals as Others in Ancient Greek Thought," *Maska* 24 (2014): 97–108, Boehrer, *Parrot Culture*, and Vincent Hunink, "An Apuleian Parrot (On Apul. *Fl.* 12)," *Acta Classica* 43 (2000): 71–9.

[55] Wynott, *Birdscapes*, 143–5, and Lyanda Lynn Haupt, *Mozart's Starling* (New York: Little Brown Spark, 2017).

[56] See Edward A. Armstrong, *A Study of Bird Song* (New York: Oxford University Press, 1963), 71.

sounds, and very often repeating what one is told by the parrot. The source of imitation is frequently lost in these relationships.[57]

Parrot learning was understood not only as a psychological or mental capacity in ancient thought, but also anatomically determined. The parrot could rise to a higher level in relation to the human than other animals could, due to the parrot's tongue. Aristotle writes, "As a general rule all birds with crooked talons are short-necked, flat-tongued, and disposed to mimicry. The Indian bird, the parrot, which is said to have a man's tongue, answers to this description" (*Historia Animalium* 597b).[58] The crucial point in the passage is the tongue, which is like a human's, and so, the parrot can speak like a human can, even if its nature tends to imitation. But so does children's nature, as a number of writers also pointed out.[59]

---

[57] Joanna Burger, *The Parrot Who Owns Me: The Story of a Relationship* (New York: Random House, 2002), describes shared domesticity with her parrot Tiko (and her husband). She writes, for example, "Early in the relationship, I could never have guessed that he was subtly training me, but in retrospect the subversive pattern is clear" (61).

Carter, *Parrot*, 8, "We persist in thinking that parrots merely mimic us, when their mimicry is a way of telling us that we are mimics. But what parrots are telling will emerge only when we listen to them differently. When communication is imagined as a net, not a cage, and the net is conceived as an architecture organizing free relations, an open web, not a more powerful technique of enslavement—only then will our symbolic and material economies be harmonized."

And see the discussion of Maxwell Knight's cuckoo in Helen Macdonald, *Vesper Flights: New and Collected Essays* (New York: Grove Press, 2020), 205–14, where Macdonald notes (213–4), "Reading Knight's book [*A Cuckoo in the House* (1955)], you sense his delight that this mysterious cuckoo has been turned, but also his disconcerted half-knowledge that it has turned into a strange, feathered proxy for Knight himself."

[58] And see Heather Dalton, Jukka Salo, Pekka Niemalä, and Simo Örmä, "Frederick II of Hohenstaufen's Australasian Cockatoo: A Symbol of Détente between East and West, and Evidence of the Ayyubid Sultanate's Global Reach," *Parergon* 35, no. 1 (2018): 35–60, here 39–40, and *The Art of Falconry Being the* De Arte Venandi cum Avibus *of Frederick II of Hohenstaufen*, ed. and trans. Casey A. Wood and F. Marjory Fyfe (Stanford: Stanford University Press, 1943; rp. Stanford: Stanford University Press, 1961), 77, "Birds with a thick and fleshy tongue endeavor to imitate the human voice and words they hear most frequently. These are chiefly the raven, the magpie family, and, still more frequently, the parrots of the green variety and even more often those of the white species. Parrots also pronounce the letter 'R' better than other birds. Vocal accomplishments are due to the form of the tongue and other portions of the vocal organs (syrinx)."

Schwartz, *The Culture of the Copy*, 143, mentions a nineteenth-century guide for keeping parrots that recommends slitting a parrot's tongue to make the speech even more fluent.

[59] See Carter, *Parrot*, 43, and 48 citing Aelian *NA* 16.2, and René Descartes, *Discourse on Method and Meditations on First Philosophy*, trans. Donald A. Cress, 4th ed. (Indianapolis: Hackett, 1998), 32–3.

The physiological similarity of humans and parrots in relation to speech capacity makes them natural models for pedagogy. As children need corporal correction, so do parrots. And the results can be similar, retention of what they are taught, good and bad. It is clear that the birds, like children, can be educated, but Apuleius and other writers would say that they can learn but not discern.[60] Parrots do not have an innate moral judgment, which humans have, he says (*Flor.* 17.18–19); they use curse words they are taught and cannot decide for themselves to speak decorously like a philosopher. Such positions are literary postures for the most part; their veracity is always deeply questionable—we've all met philosophers, after all.

Such views are found in other cultures, as well. In South Asia, the parrot has been a totem for learning, a model and guide for the acquisition of knowledge. Young students of the Veda sometimes wear the tongue of a parrot as an amulet; once they have completed their studies, they ingest the tongue and become "another talking bird."[61] That assimilation of parrot potential, here the wisdom acquired from the learning of sacred texts, is absorbed bodily, new subjects being made in education that are closer now to parrot-state. Education is the key transformer, for parrots are wise, when properly learned, and like humans, they can also be mischievous and stupid, if incompletely or insufficiently educated; they can be in South Asian traditions, "shrewd, cunning, faithful, self-sacrificing, fit for delicate missions, and capable of extricating men from difficult situations."[62] These precedents need not have been circulating in Isaac's world for him to have understandings of parrot capacities and to have considered their emulation. Indeed, his text gets there, as we'll see, in its merging and even submerging of writer's voice (and audience) with the parrot's to the degree that they all become 'talking birds'.

---

[60] See the story of the deceived parrot in *The Byzantine Sinbad. Michael Andreopoulos*, trans. Jeffrey Beneker and Craig A. Gibson, Dumbarton Oaks Medieval Library, vol. 67 (Cambridge, MA: Harvard University Pres, 2021), 25–7 (16–18). The wife whose virtue was being guarded by a parrot is tricked into believing it had been raining—the wife sprinkled water on him all night, among other ruses—and the husband no longer trusts the parrot's powers of discernment.

Such parrot stories (and others similar to it) have circulated widely. See John R. Perry, "*Monty Python* and the *Mathnavi*: The Parrot in Indian, Persian and English Humor," *Iranian Studies* 36, no. 1 (2003): 63–73.

[61] Maurice Bloomfield, "On Talking Birds in Hindu Fiction," in *Festschrift Ernst Windisch zum siebzigsten Geburtstag am 4. September 1914* (Leipzig: O. Harrassowitz, 1914), 350. And see Carter, *Parrot*, 45–51.

[62] Bloomfield, "On Talking Birds in Hindu Fiction", 353.

Isaac was surely aware, in a general way at least, of these cultural currents that circulated knowledge of parrots through the Late Antique world. Regardless of his familiarity with someone like Apuleius or Pliny, which one imagines is unlikely, he was certainly alert to the unavoidable foundations Aristotle had laid for thought in his culture.[63] That hypothetical familiarity gives contrast to Isaac's own description of his parrot's learning. This extended passage on pedagogy makes fuller sense when it is read against a backdrop of an awareness of bird training, specifically speech training for parrots, as a pain-based form of learning. And moreover, the training of young boys would surely have been familiar to him, even if only from his own experiences and from his milieu. In each case, blows and abuse constitute the proper, normal method for learning.

In contrast, Isaac's divine parrot is more than animal and indeed more than human in their capacity for both learning and discernment. This parrot is more than mimic and more than philosopher. And that nature is reproof to humans (l. 422). Whereas children need stern, painful correction and monitoring, this little bird "without punishment and bruises... chirped the teaching of each thing" (ll. 418–23). They told the story as told by the ancients, they were a venerable mimic in other words (l. 426), and they were also wholly original and unique, "But a bird such as this? A bird has never spoken, and I have not heard (anything like) this, not even from a person have I received it" (ll. 427–8). Isaac stresses this startling newness: the bird is a new voice, a new confession, a new song, a new harp, and a new sound, "Just as the praise of the angels cries out 'Holy' to the Crucified one..." (l. 445). The bird has delivered a message like angels do (a comparison we'll return to), and it is also, in this way, in the Church and among those who imitate the saints, in crying "Holy with their tongue" (l. 449).

The following passages lay on shame to those who deny this truth, and Isaac has marshaled his considerable rhetorical skill to head off his audience's denial of his experience and his interpretation of it. This parrot is not like any child or bird any of them has known or encountered. They go against all expectations of teaching any of them. Isaac embraces fully that novelty of animal encounter. That meeting is all new and shocking and

---

[63] See *Les sciences en syriaque*, ed. Émile Villey, Études syriaques, vol. 11 (Paris: Geuthner, 2014).

transforming, and Isaac is opened to it, as tries to open his listeners, too: shame on you if you cannot learn the truth better than a bird, he tells them.[64]

Parrot Exemplar

Where the learning and teaching begin and end is a strikingly uncertain threshold. The parrot was the model student, certainly, as Isaac went to some length to assert. But the parrot's facets are multiple. The parrot not only learned the divine lesson; they also taught it to Isaac, who in turn is teaching it to his audience. As he says, shame on us if we ignore it.

Philosophy needed the parrot for the reasoning, speaking subject, as we've seen in the positive and negative examples above, but pedagogy also needed the parrot for determining what real learning is. We often use 'to parrot' around lessons in a derogatory manner, to mean empty repetition without discernment, but this framing is really a disservice because a certain amount of repetition is necessary for all learning. And all our learning on some level is imitation and recombination of others' words that "remain alien because this space of learning is a space of words that belong to nobody, least of all to those who write them down."[65] Discernment is a high bar for language use, and parrots have not always been seen to clear it. However, a number of animal behaviorists have made the argument that parrot speech is not rote, but "goal-directed, novel, and referential."[66] No speech is original in any radical way, and writing does not stake a claim

---

[64] See Despret, "Inhabiting the Phonocene with Birds", 254, "What that blackbird reminded me of, or rather made me experience, in its way, was the extent to which it is important that things have importance. That we should be there, available, to receive and hear things' stubborn insistence on having importance, that we should be responsible for welcoming these importances, and not the originator of them." And "…an affect had crossed the interspecific barrier, and a common ancestral endowment open to registering importances was showing up in my wonderment."

[65] Bernhard Siegert, *Cultural Techniques: Grids, Filters, Doors, and Other Articulations of the Real*, trans. Geoffrey Winthrop-Young (New York: Fordham University Press, 2015), 59.

[66] Bar-On, "Communicative Intentions", 308, and see also Eva Meijer, *When Animals Speak: Toward an Interspecies Democracy* (New York: New York University Press, 2019), 47–50, Eva Meijer, *Animal Languages*, trans. Laura Watkinson (Cambridge, MA: MIT Press, 2019), 17–23, Jennifer Ackerman, *The Genius of Birds* (New York: Penguin, 2016), 137–68, and William A. Hillix and Duane Rumbaugh, *Animal Bodies, Human Minds: Ape, Dolphin, and Parrot Language Skills* (New York: Kluwer Academic-Plenum Publishers, 2010), 237–53.

on proprietary ownership of speech. Like parrots, we always manage and manipulate speech we've learned already.

While Isaac's encounter with the parrot is apparently quite brief, it was deeply memorable, and Isaac continued to explore the ways the parrot had touched him and remade him newly clarified doctrinally. And his goal, it appears, is to use the teaching of the parrot in his own teaching. We don't know the specific context of the sermon, but its subject matter and handling suggest the possibility of a school performance of it. We know very little also about Isaac's career and his possible role as a teacher, but the pedagogical value of such a sermon is self-evident, even if its actual social instantiation cannot be determined. The lines between liturgical and pedagogical acts are not always clear in the historical record, and the participation of audience, children, or adults implicates public teaching in either case.[67] The passages of call and response, or participatory repetition, also indicate the appeal made by a leader like Isaac to his audience for their engagement and attention.[68]

The educational context of Syriac monasteries is not well known, due to the limitation of available sources and materials. But the outline of a dynamic and engaged process is evident, wherein study and intellectual labor are not divorced from prayer and liturgy. The schoolwork emphasized tradition and careful language study among the whole community as processes by which the divine could be made directly apprehensible.[69] Isaac's own situation is not made clear by the sermon, but it appears he was a monastic leader who normally resided in Edessa. The audience then for the sermon could well have been young men (and other, older men) in

---

[67] See Susan Ashbrook Harvey, "Remembering a Larger Picture," *Journal of Orthodox Christian Studies* 3, no. 2 (2020): 215–22, and Jeffrey Wickes, *Bible and Poetry in Late Ante Antique Mesopotamia: Ephrem's Hymns on Faith* (Oakland: University of California Press, 2019), 14–23.

[68] On aspects of this absorptive experience, see Susan Ashbrook Harvey, "Women and Children in Syriac Christianity: Sounding Voices," in *The Syriac World*, ed. Daniel King (London: Routledge, 2019), 554–66, and also her *Song and Memory: Biblical Women in Syriac Tradition* (Milwaukee: Marquette University Press, 2010).

[69] See the important work by Adam H. Becker, *Fear of God and the Beginning of Wisdom: The School of Nisibis and Christian Scholastic Culture in Late Antique Mesopotamia* (Philadelphia: University of Pennsylvania Press, 2006).

his charge as an elder or leader of a community.[70] In that case, the digression on pedagogical practice has some special interest. The ardors of learning would certainly have been vivid in the listeners' minds as they heard of the natural ease by which the parrot acquired wisdom and passed it on to their own teacher. That sense of congregational empathy and engagement permitted the traversing of the ostensible animal-human divide that Isaac and parrot modelled, and that the call-and-response or participatory mode would encourage.[71]

Birds were common motifs for how the monastic life can call to young men and draw them to the life. The parrot is part of that expansion of monastic recruitment to the non-human world, too, and if not monasticism, then to godly life and faith. Theodoret of Cyrrhus writes, "Splendid in his life in these pursuits and exposed as a model of virtue for those who wished to emulate him, like some singing bird Publius drew many of his fellows into this trap of salvation (i.e. the monastic life)."[72] Isaac himself was very open to animal exemplars and encouraged his readers to consider their virtues and the lessons other creatures can teach, "See what the animals possess, if only we might find their intelligence. Learn from them understanding so that you can perfect your discernment"; and "nature is

---

[70] Some claims have been made for identifying halls, located near churches and in monastic complexes, as classrooms in the Syriac tradition. See Julie Bonnéric, "Archaeological Evidence of an Early Islamic Monastery in the Centre of al-Qusur (Failaka Island, Kuwait)," *Arabian Archaeology and Epigraphy* (2021): 1–12, and Marie-Joseph Steve, *L'île de Kharg: une page de l'histoire du Golfe Persique et du monachisme oriental* (Neuchâtel: Civilisations du Proche-Orient, 2003), 109–10; and perhaps also the building identified as a possible refectory by Timothy Insoll, Robert Carter, Salman Almahari, and Rachel MacLean, "Excavations at Samahij, Bahrain, and the Implications for Christianity, Islamisation and Settlement in Bahrain," *Arabian Archaeology and Epigraphy* 32, S1 (2021): 395–421, here 416.

[71] For the Byzantine context of such dynamics, see Andrew Mellas, *Liturgy and Emotions in Byzantium: Compunction and Hymnody* (Cambridge: Cambridge University Press, 2020), Andrew Walker White, *Performing Orthodox Ritual in Byzantium* (Cambridge: Cambridge University Press, 2015), and Alexander Lingas, "From Earth to Heaven: The Changing Musical Soundscape of the Byzantine Liturgy," in *Experiencing Byzantium: Papers from the 44th Spring Symposium of Byzantine Studies, Newcastle and Durham, April 2011*, ed. Claire Nesbitt and Mark Jackson (Farnham, Surrey: Ashgate, 2013), 311–58.

[72] Theodoret of Cyrrhus, *History of the Monks of Syria*, V, 3; trans. Richard M. Price, *A History of the Monks of Syria by Theodoret of Cyrrhus* (Kalamazoo, MI: Cistercian Publications, 1985), 59. See Shafiq Abouzayd, "Animals in Early Syrian Christian Ascetic Spirituality," *ARAM* 32, nos. 1&2 (2020): 45.

transparent, simple and straightforward, and its yoke is gentle."[73] This encouragement to read the lessons in the nonhuman world is not unusual among Late Antique writers generally, but Isaac sees the learning potential even more keenly and thoroughgoingly than those writers.

One can imagine this context, then, in which Isaac, occupying roles as both teacher and student, performs his sermon to an audience of fellow monastics, or to a lay audience, both audiences needing guidance on basic and crucial points of doctrine of the moment. The contexts can only be imagined; we can't know from this evidence where the sermon was performed or how often, but it was collected, disseminated, and read after the fact, too. It *did* have audiences. And some of the physical context can also be imagined, a church or classroom, in which Isaac's voice, crying 'Holy, Holy' again and again, perhaps encouraged his audience to join in the call and response. Perhaps even at moments like when he describes the parrot's wings stretching forth like the Crucified One and like the seraphim, Isaac would have stretched his own arms out to mimic the bird, the angels and Christ in one merging moment of imbricated bodies.

Isaac was also deeply alert to the formational qualities of sound, as he described so vividly in his sermon on the nighttime music festival at Antioch,[74] and the reverberations of 'Holy, Holy' through his sermon on the parrot in those architectural spaces surely entered into his audience with percussive, transformative force. Sharon Gerstel and colleagues have recently published a study of the effects of sound on a number of Byzantine churches in Thessaloniki, joining a growing number of sound-study scholars in the Byzantine and East Christian worlds.[75] They describe the bodied

---

[73] Homily 40, 493: 12–13, and 43, 525: 14–17; trans. Abouzayd, "Animals in Early Syrian Christian Ascetic Spirituality", 50. Isaac follows in this way the scriptural precedent of Job 12:7–9, "Ask the animals, and they will teach you, or the birds of the air, and they will tell you; or speak to the earth, and it will teach you, or let the fish of the sea inform you. Which of all these does not know that the hand of the Lord has done this?" Isaac also sees negative models in the animal world for monastic perfection; see Abouzayd, "Animals in Early Syrian Christian Ascetic Spirituality", 57–8.

[74] Again, see translation (RK) and analysis in GP, *Byzantine Media Subjects*.

[75] See Kim Haines-Eitzen, *Sonorous Desert: What Deep Listening Taught Early Christian Monks and What It Can Teach Us* (Princeton: Princeton University Press, 2022), Amy Papalexandrou, "Perceptions of Sound and Sonic Environments Across the Byzantine Acoustic Horizon," in *Knowing Bodies, Passionate Souls: Sense Perceptions in Byzantium*, ed. Margaret Mullett and Susan Ashbrook Harvey (Washington, D.C.: Dumbarton Oaks Research Library and Collection, 2017), 67–85, and the essays in *Aural Architecture in Byzantium: Music, Acoustics, and Ritual*, ed. Bissera Pentcheva (London: Routledge, 2018).

impressions of sound that we can still, to some degree, identify and measure,

> The perceived dissolution of the boundary between the terrestrial and heavenly is brought about through the engagement of the mind and the senses. Byzantine writers, notably churchmen who were witnesses to the sound and performance of liturgical prayer within decorated structures, frequently describe the intermingling of human and angelic voices within ecclesiastical settings.[76]

In these ways, we can gain some indirect insight into some of the effects of resonance and voice in these Late Antique and medieval spaces. But with Isaac, not only do we understand the merging of human and angelic voices, but we can also experience the remarkable convergence and immersion of the animal voice of the parrot into that symphony.[77] We have here a quaternity of voices, human, animal, angelic and divine, and no human stays discrete and unchanged in that convocation.

PARROT, AGENCY, AND HUMAN SPEECH

The two animals that have consistently determined (and troubled) our understandings of the animal-human divide are chimps and parrots.[78] The former are so like humans in their expressiveness, sociality, and intelligence, while the latter copy other essential aspects of the human, namely speech, and moreover, appear to manage it with will and awareness.[79] Free will is very often the criterion for policing that divide, animals being so often ruled by appetite and instinct, we think. Focusing on the views of Descartes (because he distills these biases so usefully and influentially), animals are automata, however talented and clever, and they might rise to the level of children, but only in limited ways; their lack of soul is an

---

[76] Sharon E.J. Gerstel, Chris Kyriakis, Spyridon Antonopoulos, Konstantinos T. Raptis, and James Donahue, "*Holy, Holy, Holy*: Hearing the Voices of Angels," *Gesta* 60, no. 1 (2021): 31–49, here 31.

[77] See, for example, Lorraine Daston, "Intelligences: Angelic, Animal, Human," in *Thinking with Animals: New Perspectives on Anthropomorphism*, ed. Lorraine Daston and Gregg Mitman (New York: Columbia University Press, 2005), 41–5.

[78] Johnson, *Automatic Religion*, 30–2.

[79] See Nathan Emery, *Bird Brain: An Exploration of Avian Intelligence* (Princeton: Princeton University Press, 2016).

irredeemable flaw, in his view.[80] Moreover, Spinoza cited a parrot as equal to a robot, both being creatures that speak without "mind and sense."[81] A great deal of philosophical energy has been directed at keeping that divide in place, even as many have sought to probe and undermine it, perhaps most famously Jacques Derrida in *The Animal That Therefore I Am*.[82]

However, we might look to the Enlightenment philosopher John Locke for particular ways parrots can reveal inconsistencies and ruptures in arguments around human personhood that exclude the animal.[83] In *An Essay concerning Human Understanding*, Locke quotes the memoirs of William Temple, in which he found a humorous and profound event of parrot personhood and rationality. The passage is worth quoting at length,

> I had a mind to know from Prince Maurice's own Mouth, the account of a common, but much credited Story, that I had heard from many others, of an old Parrot he had in Brasil, during his Government there, that spoke, and asked, and answered common Questions, like a reasonable Creature; so that those of his Train there, generally concluded it to be Witchery or Possession; and one of his Chaplains, who lived long afterwards in Holland, would never from that time endure a Parrot, but said, they all had a Devil in them. I had heard many particulars of this Story, and assevered by People hard to be discredited, which made me ask Prince Maurice what there was of it...[H]e told me shortly and coldly, that he had heard of such an old Parrot when he came to Brasil, and though he believed nothing of it, and 'twas a good way off, yet he had so much Curiosity as to send for it, that 'twas a

---

[80] Descartes, *Discourse on Method*, 32–3.

[81] Benedict de Spinoza, *Theological-Political Treatise*, ed. Jonathan Israel (New York: Cambridge University Press, 2007), 175, "But if anyone answers that there is indeed no need to understand God's attributes but only to believe them, quite simply, without demonstration, he is certainly talking nonsense. For invisible things, which are objects of the mind alone cannot be seen with any other eyes than through conceptual demonstration. Those people therefore who do not grasp the demonstrations, see nothing at all of these things, and therefore whatever they report from hearsay about such questions, neither affects nor indicates their minds any more than the words of a parrot or a robot which speaks without mind and sense."

[82] See Jacques Derrida, *The Animal That Therefore I Am*, trans. David Wills (New York: Fordham University Press, 2008), as well as *The Beast and the Sovereign*, ed. Michel Lisse, Marie-Louise Mallet, and Ginette Michaud, trans. Geoffrey Bennington, 2 vols. (Chicago: University of Chicago Press, 2009–11).

[83] See Johnson, *Automatic Religion*, 171–5, and Peter Walmsley, "Prince Maurice's Rational Parrot: Civil Discourse in Locke's *Essay*," *Eighteenth-Century Studies* 28, no. 4 (1995): 413–25.

very great and a very old one; and when it came first into the Room where the Prince was, with a great many Dutch-men about him, it said presently, What a company of white Men are here? They asked it what he thought that Man was, pointing at the Prince? It answered, Some General or other; when they brought it close to him, he asked it, D'ou venes vous? it answered, De Marinnan. The Prince, A qui estes vous? The Parrot, A un Portugais. Prince, Que fais tu la? Parrot, Je garde les poulles. The Prince laughed and said, Vous gardez les poulles? The Parrot answered, Ouy, moy et je scay bien faire; and made the Chuck four or five times that People use to make to Chickens when they call them.[84]

The parrot emerges here, however second- or third-hand the anecdote, as a discerning and witty participant in the otherwise-human gathering. They confuse the identity of speakers as human and animal, and they perform a remarkable mediation among the men in the room, and between animal and human. They are evidently able to respond, which is not uncommon for a parrot, but also able to pose questions, to switch from English to French (it seems), and to display a mastery over fellow birds, even to the point of mimicking human sounds made to mimic chicken sounds. It's a complex exchange, and Locke recognized it as such. It also represents a contradiction of some of his theses around the symbolic uses of signs and their manipulation in human language. But the story expands and complicates his argument, so that Locke can describe language acquisition by means of sophisticated mimicry, as children do in their development of understanding of language. It expands and complicates because it also comprises animal potential, namely parrots here and their capacity for abstraction.[85] Language and experience progress in tandem, not only for humans, but as Locke implies in his discussion of the story, perhaps most notably for parrot, who is as near-human here as can be. Such exchanges establish social- and self-agency for all speaking entities, "…people a lot of

---

[84] John Locke, *An Essay concerning Human Understanding*, ed. Peter H. Nidditch (Oxford: Clarendon, 1975), 333–4, quoting from William Temple, *Memoirs of what past in Christendom, from the War begun 1672 to the Peace concluded 1679* (London: R. Chiswell, 1691), 57–60.

[85] Locke, *An Essay concerning Human Understanding*, 334–5, "The Prince, 'tis plain, who vouches this Story, and our Author who relates it from him, both of them call this Talker a Parrot; and I ask any one else who thinks such a Story fit to be told, whether if this Parrot, and all of its kind, had always talked as we have a Prince's word for it, this one did, whether, I say, they would not have passed for a race of rational Animals, but yet whether for all that, they would have been allowed to be Men and not Parrots."

the time and some animals some of the time do operate in such a zone of language, and this represents in its socially alive way a sort of middle world for agency, as well."[86]

Another example of this slippage between speech and personhood, perhaps the best known in western literature, is Poll, the speech prothesis and parrot companion of Robinson Crusoe, in the novel of that name written by Daniel Defoe and first published in 1719. This novel has, of course, attracted extended, serious analysis, as has Poll, and they figure prominently in recent animal-studies discourse, including Derrida's animal work. Poll is a convenience for human supremacy and the near invisibility of animal agency, in writing and so also in human-made life. Derrida is critical of that position, to simplify a complicated argument, and he takes earlier philosophers to task for that essentialist position against the animal, "Kant, Heidegger, Levinas and Lacan...like Descartes, think that in contrast to us humans—a difference that is determined by this fact—the animal neither speaks nor responds, that its capacity to produce signs is foreign to language and limited or fixed by a program."[87] Locke might be said to belong to this general position, too, in that he held that the production of symbolic language in relation to experience is a defining element of the human. But we saw how the Brazilian parrot described by Temple problematized Locke's model with animal agency and complexity. Derrida would likely sympathize, but he reads western culture strongly marked by human supremacist positions. Poll is the animal deprived of voice and language, suppressed by human arrogance,

> ...still guided by the solidarity or affinity or structural attraction between *on the one hand* this autoimmune automatism that looks like the mechanics of a counter-narcissism that returns to itself only to ruin itself, to ruin the self, and *on the other hand* the production of that strange technical prothesis, a machine that turns by itself, that turns itself, and is called a wheel, [I should like, then] to note a curious contiguity in the text between a certain moment of auto-appellation that is none other than the mechanical and automatic hetero-appellation come from Poll the parrot—between *on the one hand*,

---

[86] David Gary Shaw, "The Torturer's Horse: Animals and Agency in History," *History & Theory* 52, no. 4 (2013): 146–67, here 156.

[87] Derrida, *The Beast and the Sovereign*, II: 89. In his argument, Poll emerges as a tragic figure, suppressed and diminished by human arrogance, becoming a version of his *animot*, his neologism in French for "an irreducible living word, a sort of monstrous hybrid" (among other things).

then this counter narcissistic and uncanny, *unheimlich* psittacism of auto-appellation, and *on the other* a certain return of the wheel.[88]

For Derrida, Poll is a high-profile victim of human exclusion of animal significance, a creature meaning and understanding nothing by our reckoning.[89]

Melanie Holm has made a counterargument, or at least a supplemental one, for increasing the agency of the animal in literature of that period. Poll is, after all, "the only person permitted to speak to me," as Crusoe says in the novel. They hold a privileged position over any other animal by virtue of their speech capacities, only supplanted when Friday arrives later. And in another passage, Poll is the source of uncanny encounter for Crusoe, who wakes to a doubling effect of speech when Poll speaks in the dark, which is to Crusoe a voice unsettlingly both his own and outside himself (like Freud encountering his own uncanny in his reflection in the train carriage). As Holm points out, the parrot is more than a troubling mirror. Poll expresses here sympathy and condolence in response to Crusoe, repeating "poor robin cruso, where have you been? How come you here?" And she notes Derrida's interpretation of these utterances as noise, from a creature who signifies nothing and understands nothing. The parrot, however, is able to identify Crusoe as a suffering being who needs comfort, "The parrot sympathy of *Robinson Crusoe* engages the imaginative agency of the sympathetic spectator, Robinson, so that he who puts himself in the position of a sympathizing other, Poll, creates the sympathy he receives."[90] Derrida might be essentially correct in his view of

---

[88] Derrida, *The Beast and the Sovereign*, II: 85, 86. And see Christopher GoGwilt and Melanie D. Holm, "Introduction: Parrots and Starlings," in *Mocking Bird Technologies: The Poetics of Parroting, Mimicry and Other Starling Tropes*, ed. Christopher GoGwilt and Melanie D. Holm (New York: Fordham University Press, 2018), 14–15, and Melanie D. Holm, "'O Friends, There Are No Friends': The Aesthetics of Avian Sympathy in Defoe and Sterne," in *ibid.*, 23–45.

[89] Derrida, *The Beast and the Sovereign*, II: 260, for example.
See David Wills, "Meditations for the Birds," in *Demenageries: Thinking (of) Animals After Derrida*, ed. Anne Emanuelle Berger and Marta Segarra (Amsterdam: Rodopi, 2011), 245–63, here 246, "The fact that live sound means something different to a bird than it does to a human has obviously led to a distinction between a 'dumb' animal and thinking human, rather than an interrogation concerning the definition of life. But we should perhaps think again, as Derrida advises in terms that we shall return to, think 'another thinking of life, of the living, within another relation of the living to their ipseity, to their *autos*, to their own autokinesis and reactional automaticity, to death, to technics, or to the mechanical'" (citing *The Animal That Therefore I Am*, 126).

[90] Holm, "'O Friends, There Are No Friends'", 36.

general disregard of animal voices, but apertures and entries into animals' discrete agency are there, just the same. Like Isaac, Defoe (along with his audiences) left himself open to parrot imagination and identification.[91]

Sound and Silence

The semantic play in our translation is noteworthy, that is, the range that the verb *lʿēz* (ܠܥܙ) possesses, a range that includes 'singing,' 'chirping' or 'squawking,' as we have seen. These songs of chirping are passed along the species line from human to parrot, you might say, creating an even field of sound shared by all. According to Isaac, the parrot is the Sign of God (*remza d-Allaha* [ܪܡܙܐ ܕܐܠܗܐ]), the vessel of the Spirit that Isaac is able to discern. Language is the medium for knowing God here, and across *lʿēz*, we have the speech that cross-species communication can share in.

Voice is a sign of agency in most human-constructed situations. And silence is assumed by us to be a marker of passivity, non-mind among animals. It is also a political means of suppressing and disenfranchising, not only among animals, but also among slave populations and deaf/mute people, for example. These states are related, as the nineteenth-century movements for abolition, disability, and animal rights progressed in related ways and with shared arguments.[92] Our politics has been marked from the beginning almost by this division between speech and noise, as Jean Rancière has argued,

> Apparently, nothing could be clearer than the distinction made by Aristotle in Book I of the *Politics*: the sign of the political nature of humans is constituted by their possession of the *logos*, the articulate language appropriate for manifesting a community in the *aisthesis* of the just and the unjust, as opposed to the animal *phone*, appropriate only for expressing the feelings of pleasure and displeasure.[93]

---

[91] As did Laurence Sterne in his *The Captive, from Sterne's Sentimental Journey* (1768), which describes how Yorrick lost his passport in Paris and jokes to himself about being put into the Bastille. He then walks into the street, hears "a voice which I took to be a child, which complained 'it could not get out'." He saw it was a starling hung in a little cage, "'I can't get out—I can't get out,' said the starling," and afterward he could only think of "the miseries of confinement." See Holm, "'O Friends, There Are No Friends'", 37–42.

[92] See Susan Pearson, "Speaking Bodies, Speaking Minds: Animals, Language, History," *History & Theory* 52, no. 4 (2013): 91–108.

[93] Jean Rancière, "Ten Theses on Politics," trans. Rachel Bowlby and Davide Panagia, *Theory & Event* 5, no. 3 (2001): [no pagination].

Articulate speech tells us of mind and will, and it gives full agency. While an animal creature, including humans such as slaves, women, and children, "...from which only groans or cries expressing suffering, hunger, or anger could emerge, but not actual speeches..." is consigned to non-consensual participation in a "human" polity.[94]

Speech and non-speech of parrots and humans are consistent elements in colonialist history. Making first landfall and meeting humans there, Columbus wrote, "I saw no beast of any kind in this island, except parrots." The humans he met had language, but not one he shared, and he therefore interpreted their sign-language welcome as an opening to domination, because of their lack of 'civilized' language. Their first gifts to the strange outsiders were these birds, which Columbus called parrots, but he also confused the humans and the parrots. The humans, he writes, will soon learn all that is said to them, which is a perfectly parrot-like process for him. At some level, he was equating the birds and humans as a way to deny both their humanity and introduce them into service and slavery to the new masters from Europe.[95] By the eighteenth century, the taciturnity of captured parrots was compared to 'Natives, who speak little.' Parrots

[94] See Holm, "'O Friends, There Are No Friends'", 27, "In colonial propaganda, parrot and other tropical birds similarly linked with indigenous populations that were to be contained, feminized and subdued by the enterprise of empire during 'a century which frequently drew facile parallels between Africans and parrots...and when the black male bodies most familiar to Europeans were either commodities to own or objects of spectacle'" [citing Felicity Nussbaum, *The Limits of the Human: Fictions of Anomaly, Race, and Gender in the Long Eighteenth Century* (Cambridge: Cambridge University Press, 2003), 195].
And Maggie M. Cao, "Playing Parrot: American Trompe L'oeil and Empire," *Art Bulletin* 103, no. 3 (2021): 97–124, especially 103–5 ('The Colonizer's Tongue'), on parrots also as commodities that speak.

[95] Gerald Sider, "When Parrots Learn To Talk, and Why They Can't: Domination, Deception, and Self-Deception in Indian-White Relations," *Comparative Studies in Society and History* 29, no. 1 (1987): 3–23, here 6, "His insistence that parrots were the only beasts points to, and for a moment conceals, a far more profound deception, which starts with the realization that parrots are birds that, after a fashion, can learn to talk. The natives will do the same; they are, or are soon to become for the Europeans, the parrots who 'very soon learn to say all that is said to them.' The denial of their humanity is total, or tends in that direction. But this denial is born in a lie, and remains riven with self-deceptions and contradictions, for if the first gift the native people brought were parrots, and if Columbus identifies the native people with parrots, then at some fundamental level he is deceiving himself into believing that the native people are giving (or should give) themselves over to him for delivery to his holy faith and to his king." See also Bruce T. Boehrer, "'Men, Monkeys, Lap-dogs, Parrots, Perish All!' Psittacine Articulacy in Early Modern Writing," *Modern Language Quarterly* 59, no. 2 (1998): 171–93.

were traded along the same routes as slaves in the period and were frequently conflated.[96]

Interpreting silence or taciturnity is also then fraught, when done without sufficient self-examination.[97] Silent animals can be uncanny and absolute, for example, how Peter Matthiesen described encountering a Great White Shark (from an underwater cage), "The shadow of sharks is the shadow of death, and they call forth dim ultimate fears. Yet there is something holy in their silence."[98] Silence here also means a great gap in understanding passing between animal and human, a total separation of natures. Science studies has also focused on the biases of researchers in their unexamined prejudices against meaning in silence, except meanings imputed from their own human positions.[99] And yet science- and animal-studies scholars have pushed back at this assumption that has guided so many projects that sought to (and did) confirm our superior position and our right to explain others' positions,

> In this view, wild animals are not one-dimensional participants in historical narratives onto which humans simply impose meanings or actions. Rather, both kinds of agents—humans and other animals—are simultaneously entangled together materially and discursively as they move through both space and time.[100]

Speech and silence both need inclusion, and when a bird like a parrot breaks through its silence and noise to speech (however succinctly), then it demands reckoning.

In the sermon, Isaac is attuned to the generative passages between sound and silence. From the outset, silence is a human mode, which the

---

[96] Robbins, *Elephant Slaves and Pampered Parrots*, 9–36, here 27–8, and also 112–21. See also Smith/Garlick, "A green Parrot for a good Speaker", 142–3, on parrots as metonyms for slavery, transatlantic displacement, women, and suppressed ideologies.

[97] See Miller, *In the Eye of the Animal*, 98–104, and at 104, "(The intelligent animals of these hagiographic stories) are solidly rooted in logos, even if they don't speak...(and they) depict how deeply in touch Christian holy men are with the created order."

[98] Peter Matthiessen, *Blue Meridian: The Search for the Great White Shark* (New York: Random House, 1971), 5, and 198, "For a while, the atmosphere was quiet as both sharks kept their distance from the ship; they came and went like spirits in the mist."

[99] Vinciane Despret, *What Would Animals Say If We Asked the Right Questions?* trans. Brett Buchanan (Minneapolis: University of Minnesota Press, 2016), is very persuasive.

[100] Jennifer Adams Martin, "When Sharks (Don't Attack): Wild Animal Agency in Historical Narratives," *Environmental History* 16, no. 3 (2011): 451–5, here 452.

parrot helps its human interpreter (Isaac) to shatter and to mobilize his audience similarly. Isaac asks for his silent mind to be awakened by the living word to knowledge of the Lord (l. 4). That word is delivered, in part, by the cross, the speaking pen, that allows the silent to speak (l. 9); more voices multiply in Isaac's overture to his sermon, sounding off among the lyres and harps, songs and speech initiated by the Lord. But it is also mediated by mute natures, which are made to sound and speak. Now "mute natures replied" (l. 20), and "Your cross is the key of life, which opens muzzled mouths, for the muzzled also are eloquent, with wonder they offer its glory" (ll. 71–2). Indeed, that voice ought to cause his audience shame for the better speech the parrot bears, "Let them be admonished by the silent one, for see, it confesses like someone rational; and weaving 'Holy' and praise and truth, offering to the Crucified One" (ll. 457–8).[101] The silent can speak under the new dispensation, and even noise, too, can now make sense and open up participation among all present. For Isaac, able to recognize the true speech in all that human static of the square at St. Peter's, that reckoning was with God and with his own subject state. By the end of the sermon, Isaac is pressing his audience to resist silence for the voice of the faithful bird. The parrot chirped, spoke, sang, praised, filled the silence with their better, altruistic devotion. Isaac tells us we can only hope for true faith and salvation if we switch from our heedless muteness—the parrot "dared to speak openly against a people who had silenced the prophets" (l. 733)—to that animal voice that passed into speech attending to the Lord.

Message and Medium

One could still object that the parrot is mere transmission, an innocent, disinterested mediator. Isaac is not fully decided himself about the degree to which the parrot understands their message. At times, the parrot is transmitter for the Sign, and at other times, they deliver their message as concession to creatures with greater blessings in store, but also with deeper

---

[101] Somma, "'What the Swallow Describes and the Hoopoe Reports': The Iḫwān al-ṣafā' and the Riddle of a Shared World", 110–1 on the parrot, and here 111, where the parrot also speaks infra, "And finally, the parrot highlights something human beings are unable to witness themselves, but which would overturn the human claim to superiority based on oration and eloquence. 'But if you could follow the discourse of the birds... you would realize that among these throngs are orators and eloquent speakers, theologians, preachers, admonishers, and diviners, just as there are among the sons of Adam.'"

stains of sin. Isaac certainly finds more rhetorical traction in the latter position, using the parrot's gifts to him and his audience to persuade them to change their ways and accept this fuller truth.

The messenger is traditionally said to be automaton-like, a mere unthinking transmission medium of information from one place to another—magpies and parrots and the Archangel Gabriel come to mind.[102] But what emerges from media studies is the necessary role of the messenger in determining meaning and making new subjects within that network of information transmission. Parrots in medieval literature often play the go-between, the Other in fact who translates languages and explains meaning to human subjects. Without the parrot in these stories nothing happens, in fact. As Sarah Kay writes, "Although the parrot claims to be simply a messenger, the feelings and attitudes of both humans turns out to be heavily mediated by *them*."[103] In other words, knowledge is produced by the messenger, not merely transmitted without static, alteration, or amplification.

Michel Serres wrote a profound and deeply humorous analysis of one of Hergé's Tintin stories, *The Castafiore Diamond* (published as a single volume in 1962), in which talking birds play pivotal roles. In the story, a parrot mimics the telephone and a conversation they overheard, and in this way, the reappearance of the bird's message is really a circulation, rather than a communication; the message is empty, and here, then, "A misunderstanding of the message's object, not of its interlocutors. Reception, deception. Multiply the media, put them in series…So who's responsible for: 'Rrring! Hello? I can hear you'? The parrot, of course."[104] In Serres's terms, the parrot is the parasite in the room, for him the static on the channel (as parasite also carries this meaning in French), and they receive and make new (confusing) meaning. As he argues, bird-words are the pivots by which the plot moves in this unusual story, and "Speech, so much talked about, admires itself in its magic mirror."[105] This mirror might also be held up to Isaac's sermon. Voice appears in multiple forms, circulating among humans, objects, angels, and parrot, and it is a magical delivery system of the divine. But the system is also mediated by these

---

[102] For example, see the remarks of Sybille Krämer, *Medium, Messenger, Transmission: An Approach to Media Philosophy*, trans. Anthony Enns (Amsterdam: Amsterdam University Press, 2015), 85.

[103] Kay, *Parrots and Nightingales*, 106–19, here 114–5 (*it* changed to *them*).

[104] Michel Serres, "Laughs: The Misappropriated Jewels, or a Close Shave for the Prima Donna," trans. Sam Mele and Tony Thwaites, *Art & Text* 9 (1983): 19.

[105] Serres, "Laughs", 27.

messengers, and none is more determinant than the last, the little bird. As Perry Mason says in *The Case of the Perjured Parrot* (1939), "You have a case which entirely revolves around a parrot. Casanova is the key clew to the whole affair."[106] And in that way, the messenger chooses and makes their message.

The identity and quality of the vehicle of Isaac's transformation matter, therefore. Isaac had to find that parrot. That bird arrived to meet his theological and pastoral needs just as he sought it. The parrot was the nearhuman who could most convincingly deliver this difficult news. The parrot's qualities as uncanny almost-person with speech meant that the revelation could appear to sing without self-interest.[107] The little bird presented as an objective messenger of truth. And yet that messenger was Isaac's means of self-advocacy of theology, even as the parrot provided Isaac his own voice. In the course of this long sermon, the question naturally arises, where did Isaac and parrot begin and end?

Are We Parrot?

The question of our parrot-selves is as old as the field of the academic study of religion.[108] Religion is a field closely related to anthropology, and it learned itself as a study of other cultures' beliefs and behaviors as ways,

---

[106] Erle Stanley Gardner, *The Case of the Perjured Parrot* (New York: Triangle Books, 1944), 136, and 266, "Of all the persons who had a complete alibi, the parrot was the one who had the best. The parrot was not at the scene of the shooting. That was attested to by Mrs. Winters. Therefore, the parrot couldn't have learned his speech from hearing Sabin say those words....You see, that's the trouble with teaching a parrot something to say: you never can tell how often he'll say it, or when he'll say it."

[107] Bond/Diamond, *Thinking Like a Parrot*, 139, "Parrots show intentionality in their communications, with their own independent expectations, beliefs, and desires. The result can look a lot like a theory of mind. Parrots are astute judges of animal behavior…But parrots cannot reciprocate: they cannot view people as having independent expectations, beliefs, and desires. And they cannot make inferences based on what they think is going on in someone's else's mind."

[108] See Matthews, "Why Animals and Religion Now?", Schwartz, *The Culture of the Copy*, 145–6, J. Christopher Crocker, "My Brother the Parrot," in *The Social Use of Metaphor: Essays on the Anthropology of Rhetoric*, ed. J. David Sapir and J. Christopher Crocker (Philadelphia: University of Pennsylvania Press, 1977), 164–92, Jonathan Z. Smith, "I Am a Parrot (Red)," *History of Religions* 11, no. 4 (1972): 391–413, and Theodorus P. van Baaren, "Are the Bororo Parrots or Are We?" in *Liber amicorum: Studies in Honour of Professor Dr. C.J. Bleeker. Published on the Occasion of His Retirement from the Chair of the History of Religions and the Phenomenology of Religion at the University of Amsterdam*, ed. G. Widengren et al. (Leiden: Brill, 1969), 8–13.

ultimately, to understand the human (but primarily western monotheistic man, truth be told). Parrot-human inseparability arises again with the late nineteenth-century study by Karl von den Steinen on the Amazonian peoples called the Bororó, who were said by him to claim "Wir sind araras [red parrots]." We have only the German translation of the source given, and this startling claim has led to an extensive amount of discussion about its existential ramifications. In what ways and to what degree are the Bororó parrots? Scholars approached the questions largely through the lens of distinction: could the Bororó tell the difference between themselves and the parrots? That difference is crucial for religion as a human activity performed by discrete individuals with freedom of will—the traditional standard of religion. The Bororó manipulate plumage (some 50 types have been identified) in costumes and rituals that are connected with honoring the dead and facilitating their soul passing to their next state, which seems to be, in some fashion still eluding our categories, passing to parrot state.[109] The affinity between humans and parrots is very strong indeed, and we are left understanding von den Steinen's formulation to means that the Bororó are to parrots as caterpillars are to butterflies.

Such parrot-identification is found in other segments of Brazilian society, beyond the so-called primitive and exotic, like the Bororó. With large-scale immigration from Ottoman territories to Brazil at the end of the nineteenth century, spirit-possession practices focused on Turkish spirits. "All entailed the manifestation of spirit bodies in human bodies as scenes of enchantment, healing, inspiration, luck, and revelation."[110] The most popular of these Turkish spirits was one called Mariana Turca, who conventionally was depicted as a parrot, the arará.[111]

Being human and parrot at the same moment is not a premise of these cultures, but sharing qualities and potentials within each species is always

---

[109] See Fabio Rossano Dario, "The Relationship between Bororo Indigenous and the Birds in the Brazilian Savannah," *World News of Natural Sciences* 31 (2020): 9–24, and Sonia Ferraro Dorta, "Plumária Borôro," *Suma etnológica brasileira* 3 (1987): 227–36.
Compare with the recent study by Stefan Hanß, "Feathers and the Making of Luxury Experiences at the Sixteenth-Century Spanish Court," *Renaissance Studies* 37, no. 3 (2023): 399–438.

[110] Johnson, *Automatic Religion*, 156–7.

[111] See Mundicarmo M.R. Ferretti, "The Presence of Non-African Spirits in an Afro-Brazilian Religion," in *Reinventing Religions: Syncretism and Transformation in Africa and the Americas*, ed. Sidney M. Greenfield and André Drooger (Lanham, MD: Rowman & Littlefield, 2001), 99–112.

present. Making distinctions, and maintaining them, might seem to be a necessity for species integrity (especially human), but such work is not consistent in these examples of different facets of Brazilian culture, for example. And religion perhaps is a mode shared across these creatures, too, both human, bird and other. Critical reason might also be said to be a mode of western religion. But it need not apply in the face of the uncanny, unexpected, inexplicable, like a parrot prophet in an urban marketplace. Isaac also asks, are we parrot? And the answer would have to be, like some Brazilian peoples, yes if we hope to be more godly humans.[112]

A KNOWING PARROT

We continue to look to parrots for reaching better versions of ourselves. The French novelist, Raymond Queneau, wrote a very funny, deeply affecting story (and unpredictably so), about a young girl who comes to Paris to stay with her transvestite uncle and aunt for a couple of days while her mother spends some torrid time with her new lover. It's called *Zazie dans le métro* (1959) after the winsome, potty-mouthed child, who, despite her ardent wishes, never gets into the metro. Louis Malle made a faithfully absurd film rendering in 1961, and in both versions of the story, a strong-willed parrot called Laverdure makes their mind and disapproval known. In the novel, they say it nineteen times, but in the film only twice, "tu causes, tu causes, c'est tout ce que tu sais faire," or "you talk and talk (or yakettyyak or natter on and on), that's all you know how to do."[113]

Laverdure is the antidote to almost every way we know—and talk about—parrots. Historians, writers, scientists especially, only mention

---

[112] See especially the arguments made by Matthews, "Why Animals and Religion Now?"

[113] Raymond Queneau, *Zazie in the Metro*, trans. Barbara Wright (New York: Penguin, 2001). And See Colin Gardner, "Out of the Labyrinth, into the Métro: Becoming-animal, the Waking Dream and Movements of World in Raymond Queneau and Louis Malle's *Zazie dan le métro*," in *The Animal Catalyst: Towards Ahuman Theory*, ed. Patricia MacCormack (London: Bloomsbury, 2014), 81–90, 196, and also Roland Barthes, "Zazie and Literature," in his *Critical Studies*, trans. Richard Howard (Evanston, IL: Northwestern University Press, 1972), 117–23 [= *Essais critiques* (Paris: Seuil, 1964), 125–31, here 128], who neglects Laverdure's potential but writes at 120, "[This metalanguage] is a parasitical, motionless, sententious language, which doubles the act in the same way as the fly accompanies the coach (comme la mouche accompagne le coche); instead of the language object's imperative and optative, its principal mode is the indicative, a kind of zero degree of the act intended to *represent* the real, not to change it [his italics]." Laverdure's statements affirm Barthes's assertion.

parrots on account of the "obsessive pull" of language that we 'naturally' project onto those non-human creatures.[114] Laverdure refuses to serve as echo and mirror for the humans in the story. Their vocabulary is theirs alone. It is *we* who only talk. And they call us on it: it's all we know how to do.

As Vinciane Despret has written so persuasively, we claim that language is an index of mind; speech, meaningful speech, is only possible if a rational mind motivates it—it proves mind exists (however ableist we see that proof). Parrots are the perfect birds of philosophy, because their uncanny human speech troubles and proves our own special category of rational eloquence.[115] René Descartes argued parrots can speak like we do, but they have no expression or display that reveals that they are thinking about it. In that view, they are simply machines: animals have no intelligence, but nature acts in them, like a clock; and they have souls, but basically different from the human.[116]

By way of contrast to the Cartesian position, Laverdure is an undermining of that normalized position, that they are the only rational, reasonable entity in the group. While the rest of the cast of characters is off daydreaming, fantasizing, failing to satisfy their desires or stabilize their identities—falling out of God's plan for humanity, one could say in terms closer to Isaac's—the parrot is the realistic commentator on the wayward humans around them. Granted, their *economy* of speech might be a caution against imputing mind to them—they only use this sentence—but accurate concision when speaking the truth is a virtue, always has been. See also Isaac's unprolix parrot. That parrot also served as corrective to the humans around them with a direct and straightforward assertion of truth. They are the rational parties in those settings, Paris and Antioch both.

Parrots consistently subvert the categories of human and animal, language and mind, that allow us our self-proclaimed pre-eminence in the world. It is crucial that we not write off animals as mere metaphor, for metaphor troubles all those distinctions between human and animal.[117]

---

[114] Despret, *What Would Animals Say*, 159–60, for criticism of that conventional position.
[115] Siegert, *Cultural Techniques*, 53–5.
[116] Descartes, *Discourse on Method*, 32–3.
[117] Scholarly treatment of animals in the Byzantine world often falls into the realm of metaphorical relations. (Without prejudice) see, for example, Tristan Schmidt, *Politische Tierbildlichkeit in Byzanz: Spätes 11. bis frühes 13. Jahrhundert* (Wiesbaden: Harrassowitz Verlag, 2020), and "Father and Son like Eagle and Eaglet: Concepts of Animal Species and Human Families in Byzantine Court Oration (11th/12th c.)," *Byzantinische Zeitschrift* 112, no. 3 (2019): 959–90.

It is not simply a figure of speech, and Isaac's parrot is not simply a literary conceit (even if we don't have more historical specificity than what Isaac gives us), and they are completely plausible. They are the means by which Isaac refigures his audience in speech as better humans newly opened to salvation. Laverdure is not *like* a human, a stand-in for the author's wry disdain, and not only animal, but an agent in the story who meets other creatures in the halfway, in the 'becoming'. Even if Laverdure is not able to take part directly in all the hijinks of the majority of the players, they are still a performative actor in a story where everyone is becoming-animal.[118]

Parrot is not just a literary convenience. Parrot can take on subject position, even when they are reported by someone else; and that they can be agent, and make, inspire, alter other agents.[119] They are "inhabiting zones of indistinction where traditional binary distinctions between human beings and animals break down."[120] In Laverdure, Queneau gives another kind of human, a creature that unsettles our presumption of mastery of language, mind, and world, and reveals a way to accept our instability as human subjects and for us to live into it. To quote Deleuze and Guattari, "[W]e become animal so that the animal also becomes something else."[121] Isaac's parrot is equally unsettling in its becoming so much more than a parrot might seem to be. They gave Isaac and his audience a model of righteousness to refashion themselves into more godly humans.

---

[118] Gilles Deleuze and Félix Guattari, *Kafka: Toward a Minor Literature*, trans. Dana Polan (Minneapolis: University of Minnesota Press, 1986), 22, "The thing and other things are no longer anything but intensities overrun by deterritorialized sounds or words that are following their lines of escape. It is no longer a question of a simple wordplay. There is no longer man or animal, since each deterritorializes the other, in a conjunction of flux, in a continuum of reversible intensities. Instead, it is now a question of becoming that includes the maximum of difference as a difference of intensity, the crossing of a barrier, a rising or a falling, a bending or an erecting, an accent on the word. The animal does not speak 'like' a man but pulls from the language tonalities lacking in signification; the words themselves are not 'like' the animals but in their own way climb about, bark and roam around, being properly linguistic dogs, insects, or mice."

[119] Vinciane Despret, "From Secret Agents to Interagency," *History & Theory* 52, no. 4 (2013): 29–44.

[120] Matthew Calarco, *Thinking through Animals: Identity, Difference, Indistinction* (Stanford: Stanford University Press, 2015) (no pagination).

[121] Gilles Deleuze and Félix Guattari, *What Is Philosophy?* trans. Hugh Tomlinson and Graham Burchell (New York: Columbia University Press, 1994), 109, and also Deleuze/Guattari, *Kafka*, 22, "...there is a circuit of states that forms a mutual becoming, in the heart of a necessarily multiple or collective assemblage."

Isaac's parrot is only reported by him, and yet they are vividly present not only in the story he tells, but also in the theology he creates. Indeed, the parrot is instrumental in both: without them, the story would never have begun, and without them, the particular revelation of the spread and depth of God's dispensation for creation would not have been delivered. They are a surprise actor, to be sure. Isaac *hears* them first as he comes to a crowded square before the great church of St. Peter in Antioch, and then he sees them.[122] Isaac is a masterful setter of scenes, and his homilies must have been extraordinarily persuasive performances, a trait he shared with his (sadly) unnamed parrot. And they with their masterful performance captivated him. Unlike most in that throng (maybe everyone), he was able to discern real truth in a profoundly distilled song of orthodoxy. And he was re-made in their image; Isaac was transformed, converted by their song, and we would say took part in a mutual becoming across or between species. Their parrot-state is the agent of change and metamorphosis in the homily. Becoming-animal is the proper subject position, as the parrot models and Isaac argues, for a full knowledge of the real truth of Christ's sacrifice on the cross and of its redemptive meaning. And Isaac becomes more righteous parrot-state than he knew or was able to recognize.

Parrot and the Holy Spirit

Voices circulate thoroughly and throughout the sermon. The parrot is capacious in the voices they carry. Now, they say very little, in fact. Only the speech they produced in the square does Isaac report on, though it struck him very strongly indeed. They carry within them, through them, the "living word" (l. 3) that will awaken Isaac's mind, but in the opening section, the writer likewise describes a noisy world of surprising and intermingling sound subjects, which include things, animal, human, divine: the writer's tongue is a God-inscribing pen (l. 8); the cross is a "speaking pen" that relieves silence in those not able to speak (l. 9); and instruments, like the harp and lyre, too will begin to sing hymns (l. 13). Not just speaking

---

[122] See Carter, *Parrot*, 18, "In the unexpectedness of their utterances, they are unconscious consciences." But parrots had to be enslaved to be known; they are the bad consciences of colonialism.

words, but also singing music spread across this full soundscape. This soundscape is by no means only mellifluous and filled with gentle sounds (l. 11); the combat among sounds also proceeds: demons howl (l. 12), and thieves belch forth (l. 16). The lyre of the cross, however, will overwhelm the lyre of the idol (l. 25), and the songs of praise will defeat mockery (l. 26); the sweet, living harp will capture minds and fix their bodies to the cross (ll. 29–30). From the very beginning, Isaac is layering on sounds that create a symphonic conversation among and within God's creation (though it has an operatic quality, with stage actions and lightworks, too—a *Gesamtkunstwerk* is summoned), a conversation that is broken through by the clear call of the parrot among the crowd before St. Peter's—that voice emerges, briefly but unmistakably, to Isaac, and it occupies him.

Isaac describes the moment of conversion: the parrot sang three times to affirm the truth of the Addition, pushing back against the sounds of the crowd and the idols placed there by Satan (ll. 149–52)—ironically, before St. Peter's, where speaking thrice had a resonance in the sacred past, and so animal knows truth about human again, as rooster did Peter. The bird spoke like a human—twittering, squawking, speaking, singing, whatever the mood, they were articulate and true. For Isaac, the song indeed resembled lullabies (ܢܨܪܬܐ *nusratha* [pl.] l. 156), a striking word choice, since it brings to mind children being sung to, being led to certain ways of thinking and feeling through tune and word that are chosen for their less mature, more impressionable natures. The semantic range of *nusratha* is rich: it can encompass also 'joyful hymns,' even to the 'chirping, twittering and singing of birds.' Isaac's choice of words is poetically open, and voice is travelling across a number of possible registers and moods. So, humans were then lullabied (or hymned or twittered) to by the parrot, but their "chanting" also resembled that of the seraphim, the holiest of the angelic hierarchy. For the refrain begins, and Isaac initiates a rhythmic, incantatory rendering of the parrot's speech: "Holy, Holy God," he and they repeat in a hypnotic passage of some seventy lines (ll. 57–225). The parrot is multiple here: they are also lyre and harp, beautiful singer like an angel; and they are the authentic, beautiful voice not followed by "the impure who did not (cry) holy to God as was fitting" (l. 168).[123]

The parrot is also the Sign, the Holy Spirit, the pneuma that delivers and infuses those in their vicinity. It is and arrives the divine. It is the voice presence of God, as Jesus was the bodied presence.[124] Parrots have long been confounded with the spirit in iconography, and birds, especially a dove, have frequently stood in for the incomprehensible spirit (and excited

---

[123] This aspect might be the very essence of parrot, their restless, endless multiplicity. Parrots were understood to be creatures of paradise. But, on the one hand, they could be the talking, persuasive advocate of disobedience, i.e. replacing the serpent, and thus be responsible for leading Adam and Eve astray; see Sax, *Avian Illuminations*, 135. On the other, they were also positive signs of paradise when they began to arrive in Early Modern Europe. See A.S.T. Fisher, "Birds of Paradise," *Notes and Queries* 188, no. 5 (1945): 95–8, here 96. "After the annexation of the Moluccas by the Portuguese, an extensive trade in the skins of these birds was established, the legs and true wings being carefully removed in their preparation. As all specimens reaching Europe were therefore legless, the legend arose that the birds of paradise never settled, but floated in the wind and fed upon the dews of heaven." See, also, *Albrecht Dürer's Material World*, ed. Edward H. Wouk and Jennifer Spinks (Manchester: Manchester University Press, 2023), 177, 198.

For a suggestive parallel, see José M. Capriles, Calogero M. Santoro, Richard J. George, Eliana Flores Bedregal, Douglas J. Kennett, Logan Kistler, and Francisco Rothhammer, "Pre-Columbian Transregional Captive Rearing of Amazonian Parrots in the Atacama Desert," *Proceedings of the National Academy of Sciences of the Unites States of America* 118, no. 15 (2021): 5, "Based on the identification of 27 complete or partial bird remains from five different archaeological sites, we verify pre-Columbian complex transregional circulation, captive rearing, and ritual use of translocated neotropical macaw and amazon parrots in the Atacama Desert of northern Chile. Their associated archaeological context suggests that highly elaborate and ritualized mummification processes were carried out at the time of their death and interment. In particular, all birds from known provenience were found in funerary contexts, some either wrapped or bagged in textiles and most placed in specific positions, including resting or with their beaks wide open."

[124] Mark I. Wallace, *When God Was a Bird: Christianity, Animism, and the Re-Enchantment of the World* (New York: Fordham University Press, 2019), 3, "Woven in the core grammar of Christian faith, then, is the belief in the Spirit as the *animal* face of God, even as Jesus is the *human* face of God."

theological opposition for reason of mischaracterization), as Philoxenus shows in the Introduction.[125]

Perhaps the most dramatic version of the divine presence in parrot is Gustave Flaubert's novella "A Simple Heart (*Un coeur simple*)," published in 1877.[126] The principal character in the novel, besides the parrot Loulou, is the housemaid Félicité, possessor of the simple heart of the title. The family keeps a live parrot, who becomes Félicité's companion, to the point that, following the bird's demise, she has them stuffed and installed in her rooms. The unimaginable nature of the Holy Spirit for Félicité, who is deeply pious, causes her puzzlement, which is resolved by Loulou. Their brilliant appearance ("Their body was green, the tips of their wings were pink, their head blue, and their breast golden") and speech ("Nice boy! Your servant, sir! Hail, Mary!") lead her to invest the (now stuffed) parrot with divine agency,

> In church, she was forever gazing at the Holy Ghost, and one day she noticed that it had something of the parrot about it. This resemblance struck her as even more obvious in a colour-print depicting the baptism of Our Lord. With its red wings and its emerald-green body, it was the very image of Loulou…They were linked together in her mind, the parrot being sanctified by the connection with the Holy Ghost, which themself acquired new life and meaning in her eyes. God the Father could not have chosen a dove as a means of expressing Himself, since doves cannot talk, but rather

---

[125] See Glenn Peers, *Subtle Bodies: Representing Angels in Byzantium* (Berkeley: University of California Press, 2001), 71–4. And see Bruce T. Boehrer, "The Cardinal's Parrot: A Natural History of Reformation Polemic," *Genre* 41 (2008): 1–37, Richard Verdi, *The Parrot in Art from Dürer to Elizabeth Butterworth* (London: Scala, 2007), and Heather Dalton, "A Sulphur-Crested Cockatoo in Fifteenth-Century Mantua: Rethinking Symbols of Sanctity and Patterns of Trade," *Renaissance Studies* 28, no. 5 (2013): 676–94, here 683, "Because a parrot is able to relay a spoken message without attempting to interpret, alter or add to it, it was seen as a reliable messenger of revelation and became associated with the Annunciation."
And see the Introduction for Philoxenus and doves.

[126] Gustave Flaubert, "A Simple Heart," in *Three Stories*, trans. Robert Baldick (Harmondsworth: Penguin, 1961), 17–56, and see the brilliant, ruminative study of Julian Barnes, *Flaubert's Parrot* (New York: Random House, 1985). See also Siegert, *Cultural Techniques*, 63–7, Julia Courtney, "The View from the Perch: Flaubert's Loulou," in *The Role of the Parrots in Selected Texts from Ovid to Jean Rhys*, 87–110, Boehrer, *Parrot Culture*, 100–5, 121–3, and Schwartz, *The Culture of the Copy*, 144.

one of Loulou's ancestors. And although Félicité used to say her prayers with her eyes on the picture, from time to time she would turn slightly towards the bird.[127]

The transposition of bird to spirit becomes total for her, as she ages and nears death. The glass eye of the parrot reflects light in a way that sent her into ecstasies of prayer, and the final line of the novella completes the bird's apotheosis, "And as she breathed her last, she thought she could see, in the opening heavens, a gigantic parrot hovering above her head."[128]

Possession by parrot is a frequent element in those who attempt to write about them, and therefore know and share something of them. Flaubert was evidently preoccupied with his parrot creation and kept a taxidermic reminder near him as he composed the novella, as he noted in a letter of July 1876, "A stuffed parrot. It sits there on sentry duty. The sight of it is beginning to irritate me. But I keep it there so that I can fill my head with the idea of parrothood."[129] Parrots are not undemanding companions, living or dead, but it was clear that the parrot, as such, inspired Flaubert (in the sense of the Holy Spirit, one might say) and dictated the story, as occupying voice.[130] Julian Barnes writes, after all, "Is the writer much more than a sophisticated parrot?"[131] In that vein, then, Isaac is (as already noted) parroting the parrot, spoken by them and made godly in their image. As is the audience for the sermon, as they potentially join

---

[127] Flaubert, "A Simple Heart", 44, 50 (translation de-gendered).
[128] Flaubert, "A Simple Heart", 56.
In a different, but related mode, see Jorge Comensal, *The Mutations*, trans. Charlotte Whittle (New York: Farrar, Straus & Giroux, 2019), which ends with Elodia—the maid who gave the dying Ramón a parrot called Benito—allowing Ramón to die in the company of the speaking Benito: "Elodia murmured a hodgepodge of prayers, while Benito paid jubilant tribute to Ramón's life. 'Lamb of God...' 'Son of a bitch!'
'...You take away the sins of the world...' 'Son of a bitch!' 'only say the word and my soul shall be healed...' What the fuck? Son of a bitch!' Ramón opened his mouth like a hungry chick seeking its mother." The parrot's 'benediction' ushers the ecstatic Ramón across the threshold of death.
[129] Barnes, *Flaubert's Parrot*, 184.
[130] Barnes, *Flaubert's Parrot*, 19, "The parrot/writer feebly accepts language as something received, imitative and inert. Sartre himself rebuked Flaubert for passivity, for belief (or collusion in the belief) that *on est parlé*—one is spoken."
[131] Barnes, *Flaubert's Parrot*, 18.

the recitation of Holy Holy, the point being to persuade them to repeat after me (Isaac, parrot), as it were, to speak the new, proper prayer.[132]

Becoming Parrot

Isaac's own conversion is complete.[133] If he had been wavering or been unconvinced of the necessity of the Addition, the bird won him over. But it was not only a conversion of theological reasoning. Isaac also fell into this position against the defilers in the square through a possession of a new voice that the rhythmic repetition of parrot words reveals. The "holy, holy God" refrain begins as a report of the bird's true confession, but it submerges into Isaac's own voice, as he repeats it again and again in a powerful recitation of the cross-centered sacrifice of God made flesh. Here, then, animal-human come to share the same adhesion (the same becoming) to the revelation of God's will in the crucifixion, but the animal was there first, reminded Isaac of the words, and led him to expansive insights into the words and their ramifications for redemption.

The bird is "a new idea," "a new confession," "a new song," "a new harp," a new sound (ll. 429–39). They are assimilated by voice to the cross, the Lord, the seraphim, and their small body, likewise, formed to the sacred. When they spread their wings (ll. 461–6), they depicted the mysteries of the cross in their body shape; the cross was inscribed on them. And at the same moment, their voice sang out faith and truth. This enfolding of cross, person, and animal together recalls the use of "shared embodiment" by Patricia Miller in her examination of talking animals as ways to advertise "their mutual embeddedness in a matrix that is both

---

[132] Siegert, *Cultural Techniques*, 67, "As the writer turns into a parrot, humans are transformed into channels directly linking god and animal. Flaubert returns the difference between bird speech and human language, thereby exchanging his role as author with that of secretary or parrot. A parrot that reveals human speech as an assemblage of commonplaces, a variant of parrot discourse, which deserves to be silenced. A parrot as the truth and end of all speech."
Laverdure's accusation stands: all we do is natter on.
[133] On becoming: Smith/Garlick, "'A green Parrot for a good Speaker'", 148–50. On conversion: Gerald L. Bruns, "Becoming-Animal (Some Simple Ways)," *New Literary History* 38, no. 4 (2007): 704, "Becoming is a pure event, a simultaneity 'whose characteristic is to elude the present. Insofar as it eludes the present, becoming does not tolerate the separation or the distinction of before and after, or of past and future. It pertains to the essence of becoming to move and to pull in both directions at once'" [citing Gilles Deleuze, *The Logic of Sense*, trans. Mark Lester (New York: Columbia University Press, 1990), 1].

corporeal and spiritual...Further, when the binary between human and animal is destabilized, so is that between matter and spirit."[134] There has to be some charm and wit that Isaac is applying to his recounting of this powerful moment—the contrast of this little performing bird to the immensity of their insights is so striking—but that does not make the lessons less affecting, persuasive, and momentous here.

In this small body and voice, Isaac found a subject position that clarified the difficult issues at stake and gave him a voice he could use in good conscience. And he did in this sermon. He entered into their voice, ventriloquized the parrot (and was ventriloquized), because they embodied a Sign of truth. By the end, Isaac is enjoining his listeners to become, like the parrot, temple trumpets (ll. 1043–4), true laborers (ll. 1045–6), and living trumpets (ll. 1047–8), for life, mind, and soul, were spread across all creation in the ocean of sound submerging all who would hear Holy, Holy. Humans have been given a different order of expectation by God, and the parrot confounded it by stating more truly the revelation of God. The bird's position is so much more laudable for their lack of expectation of salvation—without hope of reward themselves, they were a real figure of emulation. The little parrot is more than imitative speech: they are a messenger, like an angel; they are more than the play-back language machine of Descartes; and they perform revelation in their Sign from the Holy Spirit. And so, Isaac tells his audience to be like a laborer in the service of God, but also be an instrument, be an animal. Be. Don't just yakkety yakyak. Use becoming-animal for a mutually formed godly assemblage, as Deleuze and Guattari might say (except for godly).[135] Or like Wittgenstein's lion, perhaps we should work at looking more closely at our ignorance, accept the existence of other, animal minds, as Isaac tried, and overcome our own need to play God, like overweening Hanno who was thwarted by his freed, free-willed birds so long ago.[136]

---

[134] Miller, *In the Eye of the Animal*, 89, but see 86–98 broadly.

[135] And they would also say, "That is why the distinction we must make is less between kinds of animals than between the different states according to which they are integrated into family institutions, State apparatuses, war machines, etc. (and what is the relation of the writing machine and the musical machine to becomings-animal?)." As they did in *A Thousand Plateaus: Capitalism and Schizophrenia*, trans. Brian Massumi (Minneapolis: University of Minnesota Press, 1987), 243.

[136] See Cary Wolfe, "In the Shadow of Wittgenstein's Lion: Language, Ethics, and the Question of the Animal," in *Zoontologies: The Question of the Animal*, ed. Cary Wolfe (Minneapolis: University of Minnesota Press, 2003), 1–57, here 2–3. The dictum is "If a lion could talk, we could not understand him."

Select Bibliography

AbouZayd, Shafiq. "Animals in Early Syrian Christian Ascetic Spirituality." *ARAM* 32, nos. 1&2 (2020): 31–60.
AbouZayd, Shafiq. "Isaac of Antioch on Learning and Knowledge." In *VI Symposium Syriacum, 1992: University of Cambridge, Faculty of Divinity, 30 August – 2 September 1992*, ed. René Lavenant, 215–20. Orientalia Christiana Analecta, vol. 247. Roma: Pontificio Istituto Orientale, 1994.
Barnes, Julian. *Flaubert's Parrot*. New York: Random House, 1985.
Bar-On, Dorit. "Communicative Intentions, Expressive Communication, Origins of Meaning." In *The Routledge Handbook of Philosophy of Animal Minds*, ed. Kristin Andrews and Jacob Beck, 301–12. Abingdon: Routledge, 2017.
Baumstark, Anton. "Altsyrische Profandichtung in gereimten Siebensilbern." *Orientalische Literaturzeitung* 36 (1933) 343–48.
Bedjan, Paul. *Homiliæ S. Isaaci, Syri Antiocheni*. Leipzig: Otto Harrassowitz, 1903.
Bickell, Gustav. *Ausgewählte Gedichte der syrischen Kirchenväter: Cyrillonas, Baläus, Isaak von Antiochien und Jakob von Sarug, zum ersten Male aus dem Syrischen übersetzt*. Bibliothek der Kirchenväter, vol. 12. Kempten: Kösel, 1872.
Bickell, Gustav. *Sancti Isaaci Antiocheni, doctoris Syrorum, opera omnia*. Giessen: J. Ricker, 1873.
Bloomfield, Maurice. "On Talking Birds in Hindu Fiction." In *Festschrift Ernst Windisch zum siebzigsten Geburtstag am 4. September 1914*, 349–61. Leipzig: O. Harrassowitz, 1914.

Boehrer, Bruce T. *Parrot Culture: Our 2500-Year-Long Fascination with the World's Most Talkative Bird*. Philadelphia: University of Pennsylvania Press, 2004.
Bond, Alan B.; and Judy Diamond. *Thinking Like a Parrot: Perspectives from the Wild*. Chicago: University of Chicago Press, 2019.
Bou Mansour, Tanios. "Une clé pour la distinction des écrits des Isaac d'Antioche." *Ephemerides Theologicae Lovanienses* 79, no. 4 (2003): 365–402.
Bou Mansour, Tanios. "La distinction des écrits d'Isaac d'Antioche: les œuvres inédites." *Journal of Eastern Christian Studies* 57, nos. 1–2 (2005a): 1–46.
Bou Mansour, Tanios. "Les discours à caractère christologique et leur appartenance aux Isaac (d'Antioche)." *Oriens Christianus* 89 (2005b): 8–42.
Bou Mansour, Tanios. "Les écrits ascétiques ou "monastiques" d'Isaac dit d'Antioche." *Journal of Eastern Christian Studies* 57, nos. 1–2 (2007): 49–84.
Brock, Sebastian P. "The Published Verse Homilies of Isaac of Antioch, Jacob of Serug, and Narsai: Index to Incipits." *Journal of Semitic Studies* 32, no. 2 (1987): 279–313.
Brock, Sebastian P. "A Soghitha on the Upright Jephtha and on His Daughter, by Mar Isaac." In *Jacob of Sarug's Homily on Jephthah's Daughter*, ed. Susan Ashbrook Harvey and Ophir Münz-Manor, 63–9. Texts from Christian Late Antiquity, vol. 22, Homilies of Mar Jacob of Sarug, vol. 16. Piscataway, NJ: Gorgias Press, 2010.
Brock, Sebastian P. "A Soghitha on the Daughter of Jephtha, by Isaac." *Hugoye: Journal of Syriac Studies* 14, no. 1 (2011): 3–25.
Brock, Sebastian P. "An Acrostic Soghitha by Isaac 'the Teacher' in Sinai Syr. 10." *Collectanea Christiana Orientalia* 12 (2015): 47–62.
Carter, Paul. *Parrot*. London: Reaktion, 2006.
Chakhtoura, Elias. "Il digiuno nella tradizione della Chiesa siriaca antica: I mīmrē al-sawmō nel corpus di Isacco d'Antiochia." Dissertatio ad doctoratum, Pontificium Institutum Orientale, Facultas Scientiarum Ecclesiasticarum Orientalium, 2014.
Chakhtoura, Elias. *Il digiuno nella tradizione della Chiesa siriaca antica: I Mīmrē 'al Ṣawmō nel Corpus di Isacco d'Antiochia*. Faculté des sciences religieuses et orientales, vol. 2. Kaslik: Presses de l'Université Saint-Esprit de Kaslik, 2016.
Chakhtoura, Elias. "Fasting according to Two Syriac Church Fathers, John of Apamea and Isaac of Antioch." *ARAM* 32 (2020): 83–98.
De Giorgi, Andrea U.; and A. Asa Eger. *Antioch: A History*. London: Routledge, 2021.
Deleuze, Gilles; and Félix Guattari. *Kafka: Toward a Minor Literature*. Trans. Dana Polan. Minneapolis: University of Minnesota Press, 1986.
Derrida, Jacques. *The Animal That Therefore I Am*. Trans. David Wills. New York: Fordham University Press, 2008.
Derrida, Jacques. *The Beast and the Sovereign*. Ed. Michel Lisse, Marie-Louise Mallet, and Ginette Michaud. Trans. Geoffrey Bennington. 2 vols. Chicago: University of Chicago Press, 2009–11.

Descartes, René. *Discourse on Method and Meditations on First Philosophy.* Trans. Donald A. Cress. 4th ed. Indianapolis: Hackett, 1998.
Despret, Vinciane. "Inhabiting the Phonocene with Birds." In *Critical Zones: The Science and Politics of Landing on Earth*, ed. Bruno Latour and Peter Weibel, trans. Chris Turner, 254–9. Karlsruhe: ZKM-Cambridge, MA: MIT Press, 2020.
Despret, Vinciane. *What Would Animals Say If We Asked the Right Questions?* Trans. Brett Buchanan. Minneapolis: University of Minnesota Press, 2016.
Féghali, Paul. "Isaac d'Antioche, poème sur l'incarnation du Verbe." *Parole de l'Orient* 10 (1981–1982): 79–102.
Féghali, Paul. "Isaac d'Antioche, une hymne sur l'Incarnation." *Parole de l'Orient* 11 (1983): 201–22.
Flaubert, Gustave. "A Simple Heart." In *Three Stories*, trans. Robert Baldick, 17–56. Harmondsworth: Penguin, 1961.
Ford, Simon; and Kristy Stewart. "A Feathered Thing Happened on the Way to the Agora: A Syriac Variant of the Ancient Greek Sphinx Story." Forthcoming.
Furlani, Giuseppe. "Tre discorsi metrici d'Isacco d'Antiochia sulla fede." *Rivista trimestrale di studi filosofici e religiosi* 4, no. 3 (1923): 257–87.
Furlani, Giuseppe. "La psicologia d'Isacco d'Antiochia." *Giornale critico della filosofia italiana* 7 (1926): 241–53.
Gharib, Antonios. "Saint Isaac of Antioch's Homily on 'The Love of Learning': Translation and Commentary." *Syriac Orthodox Patriarchal Journal* 58 (2020): 1–29.
Glenthøj, Johannes Bartholdy. *Cain and Abel in Syriac and Greek Writers (4th–6th Centuries).* Corpus Scriptorum Christianorum Orientalium, vol. 567, Subs. 95. Louvain: Peeters, 1997.
Graffin, François. "Isaac d'Amid et Isaac d'Antioche." In *Dictionnaire de spiritualité ascétique et mystique: doctrine et histoire.* Paris: Beauchesne, 1971.
Greatrex, Geoffrey. "Isaac of Antioch and the Sack of Beth Hur." *Le Muséon* 111, nos. 3–4 (1998): 287–91.
Hinchliffe, Steve. "Sensory Biopolitics: Knowing Birds and a Politics of Life." In *Humans, Animals and Biopolitics: The More-Than-Human Condition*, ed. Kristin Asdal, Tone Druglitrø, and Steve Hinchliffe, 152–70. London: Routledge, 2017.
Holm, Melanie D. "'O Friends, There Are No Friends': The Aesthetics of Avian Sympathy in Defoe and Sterne." In *Mocking Bird Technologies: The Poetics of Parroting, Mimicry and Other Starling Tropes*, ed. Christopher GoGwilt and Melanie D. Holm, 23–45. New York: Fordham University Press, 2018.
Johnson, Paul Christopher. *Automatic Religion: Nearhuman Agents of Brazil and France.* Chicago: University of Chicago Press, 2021.
Kay, Sarah. *Parrots and Nightingales: Troubadour Quotations and the Development of European Poetry.* Philadelphia: University of Pennsylvania Press, 2013.

Kazan, Stanley. "Isaac of Antioch's Homily against the Jews: The Attitude towards the Jews in Syriac Literature." Unpublished Doctoral Dissertation, Yale University, 1959.

Kazan, Stanley. "Isaac of Antioch's Homily against the Jews." *Oriens Christianus* 45 (1961): 30–53; 46 (1962): 87–98; 47 (1963): 89–97; 49 (1965): 57–78.

Kessel, Grigory; and Karl Pinggéra. *A Bibliography of Syriac Ascetic and Mystical Literature*. Eastern Christian Studies, vol 11. Leuven: Peeters, 2011.

Klugkist, Alex C. "Pagane Bräuche in den Homilien des Isaak von Antiocheia gegen die Wahrsager." In *Symposium Syriacum, 1972: célebré dans les jours 26–31 octobre 1972 à l'Institut Pontifical Oriental de Rome*, ed. Ignatius Ortiz de Urbina, 353–68. *Orientalia Christiana Analecta*, vol. 197. Rome: Pontificium Institutum Orientalium Studiorum, 1974.

Klugkist, Alex C. "Die beiden Homilien des Isaak von Antiocheia über die Eroberung von Bet Hur durch die Araber." In *IV Symposium Syriacum, 1984: Literary Genres in Syriac Literature (Groningen – Oosterhesselen 10–12 September)*, ed. Hans J.W. Drijvers, René Lavenant, Corrie Molenberg, and Gerrit J. Reinink, 237–56. *Orientalia Christiana Analecta*, vol. 229. Rome: Pontificium Institutum Studiorum Orientalium, 1987.

Koch, Hugo. "Isaac von Antiochien als Gegner Augustinus." *Theologie und Glaube* 1 (1909): 622–34.

Krüger, Paul. "Der dem Isaac von Antiochien zugeschriebene Sermo über den Glauben." *Ostkirchliche Studien* 1 (1952a): 46–54.

Krüger, Paul. "Die mariologischen Anschauungen in den dem Isaak von Antiochien zugeschriebenen Sermones. Ein dogmengeschichtlicher Beitrag." *Ostkirchliche Studien* 1 (1952b): 123–31.

Krüger, Paul. "Gehenna und Scheol in dem Schrifttum unter dem Namen des Isaak von Antiochien. Ein dogmengeschichtlicher Beitrag zur Eschatologie der ältesten Zeit." *Ostkirchliche Studien* 2 (1953): 270–79.

Landersdorfer, Simon. *Ausgewählte Schriften der syrischen Dichter: Cyrillonas, Baläus, Isaak von Antiochien und Jakob von Sarug*. Bibliothek der Kirchenväter, vol. 6. Kempten: Kösel, 1913.

Locke, John. *An Essay concerning Human Understanding*. Ed. Peter H. Nidditch. Oxford: Clarendon, 1975.

Mathews, Edward George, Jr. "The Rich Man and Lazarus: Almsgiving and Repentance in Early Syriac Tradition." *Diakonia* 22 (1988–1989): 89–104.

Mathews, Edward George, Jr. "'On Solitaries,' Ephrem or Isaac?" *Le Muséon* 103 (1990): 91–110.

Mathews, Edward George, Jr. "A Bibliographical Clavis to the Corpus of Works Attributed to Isaac of Antioch." *Hugoye: Journal of Syriac Studies* 5, no. 1 (2002).

Mathews, Edward George, Jr. "The Works Attributed to Isaac of Antioch: A[nother] Preliminary Checklist." *Hugoye: Journal of Syriac Studies* 6, no. 1 (2003): 51–76.

Mathews, Edward George, Jr. "Isaac of Antioch and the Literature of Adam and Eve." In *Things Revealed: Studies in Early Jewish and Christian Literature in Honor of Michael E. Stone*, ed. Esther G. Chazon, David Satran, and Ruth A. Clements, 331–44. Journal for the Study of Judaism, Supplement Series, vol. 89. Leiden: Brill, 2004.

Mathews, Edward George, Jr. "What Manner of Man? Early Syriac Reflections on Adam." In *Syriac and Antiochian Exegesis and Biblical Theology for the 3rd Millennium*, ed. Robert D. Miller, 115–49. Gorgias Eastern Christian Studies, vol. 6. Piscataway, NJ: Gorgias Press, 2008.

Matthews, Paul Robert. "Why Animals and Religion Now?" *Humanimalia* 9, no. 1 (2018): 68–91.

Miller, Patricia Cox, *In the Eye of the Animal: Zoological Imagination in Ancient Christianity*. Philadelphia: University of Pennsylvania Press, 2018.

Moriggi, Marco. "'And the Impure and Abominable Priests Fled for Help to the Names of the Devils': Amulets and Magical Practices in Syriac Christian Culture between Late Antiquity and the Modern World." *Hugoye: Journal of Syriac Studies* 19, no. 2 (2016): 371–84.

Moss, Cyril. "Isaac of Antioch, Homily on the Royal City." *Zeitschrift für Semitistik* 7 (1929): 295–306; 8 (1930): 61–72.

Peers, Glenn. *Animism, Materiality and Museums: How Do Byzantine Things Feel?* Leeds: ARC Humanities Press, 2021.

Peers, Glenn. *Byzantine Media Subjects*. Ithaca: Cornell University Press, 2024.

Robbins, Louise E. *Elephant Slaves and Pampered Parrots: Exotic Animals in Eighteenth-Century Paris*. Baltimore: Johns Hopkins University Press, 2002.

The Role of the Parrots in Selected Texts from Ovid to Jean Rhys: Telling a Story from an Alternative Viewpoint. Ed. Julia Courtney and Paula James. Lewiston: Edwin Mellen Press, 2006.

Sax, Boria. *Avian Illuminations: A Cultural History of Birds*. London: Reaktion, 2021.

Schwartz, Hillel. *The Culture of the Copy: Striking Likenesses, Unreasonable Facsimiles*. New York: Zone Books, 1996.

Serres, Michel. "Laughs: The Misappropriated Jewels, or a Close Shave for the Prima Donna." Trans. Sam Mele and Tony Thwaites. *Art & Text* 9 (1983): 14–28.

Siegert, Bernhard. *Cultural Techniques: Grids, Filters, Doors, and Other Articulations of the Real*. Trans. Geoffrey Winthrop-Young. New York: Fordham University Press, 2015.

Smith, A.J.; and B. Garlick. "'A green Parrot for a good Speaker': Writing with a Birds-Eye View in Eliza Haywood's *The Parrot*." In *Animal Satire*, ed. Robert McKay and Susan McHugh, 137–53. Cham: Palgrave Macmillan, 2023.

The Syriac World. Ed. Daniel King. London: Routledge, 2019.

van Esbroeck, Michel. "The Memra on the Parrot by Isaac of Antioch." *Journal of Theological Studies* 47 (1996): 464–76.

van Esbroeck, Michel. "L'implication eucharistique dans le milieu antichalcédonien." In *The Eucharist in Theology and Philosophy: Issues of Doctrinal History in East and West from the Patristic Age to the Reformation*. Ed. István Perczel, Réka Forrai, and György Geréby, 67–79. Ancient and Medieval Philosophy I.35. Leuven: Leuven University Press, 2005.

van Vossel, Vincent. "Le moine syriaque et son diable." In *Le monachisme syriaque aux premieres siècles de l'Eglise, IIe – debut VIIe siècle. I: Textes français*, 191–215. Patrimoine Syriaque, Actes du Colloque V. Antélias, Lebanon: Centre d'Études et de Recherches Orientales, 1998.

Vergani, Emidio. "L'omelia sul pappagallo: l'esegesi in un testo di Isacco di Antiochia." In *La tradizione cristiana Siro-occidentale (V-VII secolo). Atti del 4° Incontro sull'Oriente Cristiano di tradizione siriaca (Milano, Biblioteca Ambrosiana, 13 maggio 2005)*, ed. Emidio Vergani and Sabino Chialà, 129–57. Milan: Centro Ambrosiano, 2007.

Vööbus, Arthur. "Beiträge zur kritischen Sichtung der asketischen Schriften die unter dem Namen Ephraem des Syrers überliefert sind." *Oriens Christianus* 39 (1955): 48–55.

Vööbus, Arthur. *History of Asceticism in the Syrian Orient: A Contribution to the History of Culture in the Near East*. Corpus Scriptores Christianorum Orientalium, vols. 184, 197, 500; Subs. 14, 17, 81. Louvain: Secrétariat du CorpusSCO, 1958, 1960, 1988.

Zingerle, Pius. "Über und aus Reden von zwei syrischen Kirchenvätern über das Leiden Jesu (Isaak von Antioch und Jakob von Serug)." *Theologische Quartalschrift* 52 (1870): 92–114; 53 (1871): 409–26.

Index[1]

A

Addition, 4, 8–11, 13–19, 40, 70, 74, 86, 113, 117
Aelian, 80, 81
Aksenāyā, 10
Allora, Jennifer, 66n9
Angelic status, parrots, 67, 85
Angels, 31, 40, 52, 54, 71, 73, 85, 92, 96, 106, 114, 118
Animal-human difference, 71
Animal studies, v, 67
Anti-Chalcedonian, 9, 13, 16
Antioch, 2–4, 8–11, 15, 20, 26, 28, 37n31, 61, 69, 70n17, 84, 96, 110, 112
Apuleius, 89, 91, 92
Aristotle, 65, 76n24, 77, 90, 92, 102
Assemani, Giuseppe Simone, 5
Athanasius of Alexandria, 77
Augustus, 81, 81n34

B

Basil I, 82
Becoming-animal, 67, 74, 111, 118
Bedjan, Paul, 6, 7n18, 21n36
Benjamin, Walter, 77
Bickell, Gustavus, 5
Bond, Alan B., 75
Bororó, 85, 108

C

Call-and-response, 16, 21, 94–96
Calzadilla, Guillermo, 66n9
Children, 29, 35, 88, 90–92, 94, 97, 99, 103, 113
Chimps, 97
Chirped, 19, 23, 26, 30, 38–41, 59–61, 70, 73, 74, 92, 105
Chirping, 3, 16, 21, 28, 34, 39, 69, 70, 102, 113
Chirps, 40–42, 73

[1] Note: Page numbers followed by 'n' refer to notes.

Christology, 4, 13
Chronica Minora, 2, 2n3, 3
Cloud of Witnesses, 13, 14, 20, 21, 46, 73
Columbus, Christopher, 103, 103n95
Comensal, Jorge, 116n128
Cross, 8–10, 13, 14, 17–19, 22, 23, 26–28, 26n2, 30–32, 34, 36, 40, 41, 44, 45, 47, 48, 53, 59, 60, 68–70, 72, 102, 105, 112, 117
Crucified, 22
Crucified One, 23, 33, 40, 96, 105
Crucifixion, 10, 19, 23, 27, 29–31, 33, 37, 40, 42, 117
Crusoe, 100, 101
Ctesias, 80

D
Defoe, Daniel, 100
Deleuze, Gilles, 118
Derrida, Jacques, 98, 100, 101, 101n89
Descartes, René, 90n59, 97, 98n80, 100, 110, 110n116, 118
Despret, Vinciane, 110
Diamond, Judy, 75
Discernment, 28, 80, 84, 86–88, 91n60, 92, 93, 95
Dove, 1–4

E
Ecclessiastes, 83
Exemplarity, 76, 84

F
Fetus, 17, 32, 58, 59, 73, 85
Flaubert, Gustave, 115, 116, 116n131

G
Gerstel, Sharon, 96

H
Hanno, 81, 84, 89, 118
Harp, 15, 19, 26, 27, 31, 33, 40, 41, 45, 72, 73, 92, 112, 113, 117
Hebrews, 20, 21, 49
Holm, Melanie, 101
Holy, Holy, 11, 15–23, 31–33, 37, 40, 42, 70, 73, 96, 113, 118
Holy Spirit, 3, 60, 61, 74, 112–118
Human-animal distinctions, 1
Human-parrot, vii
Humboldt, Alexander, 89

I
Idols, 10, 16, 26, 27, 30, 50, 51, 53, 55, 70, 113
Imitation, 32, 33, 48, 74, 90, 93
Isaac of Amid, 4
Isaac of Antioch, v, 2, 4–6, 11, 13, 26, 64
Isaac of Edessa, 4
Isaiah, 42, 42n35, 49, 73, 76, 83

J
Jacob of Edessa, 4
Jacob of Serugh, 21
Johnson, Scott F., 5

K
Kay, Sarah, 75, 106
Kosiński, Rafał, 9, 9n22
Kubrick, Stanley, 74, 75

L

Lamy, T. J., 5
Language, v, vi, 2, 3, 12, 23, 37, 64, 66n9, 79, 80, 82, 83, 85, 89, 93, 94, 99, 100, 102, 103, 109n113, 110, 111, 111n118, 118, 118n136
Laverdure, 109–111, 109n113
Leo VI, 82
Leo IX, 81
Livistros and Rodamni, 78
Locke, John, 98–100, 98n83, 99n84, 99n85
Logos, 10
Long, Thomas, 21
Loulou, 115
Lullaby, 31, 70, 113
Lyre, 15, 26, 27, 31, 33, 50, 68, 70, 112, 113

M

Malle, Louis, 109
Mariana Turca, 108
Mason, Perry, 107
Mathews, Edward G., Jr., 5, 6n13
Matthiesen, Peter, 104
Media studies, v, 106
Medium, 105–107
Mēmrā, 2–4, 7–9, 11, 13–16, 20–23, 20n35, 26, 31n12, 61
Message, 68, 73, 92, 105–107, 115n125
Messenger, 86, 106, 107, 115n125, 118
Miaphysite, 3, 4, 10–13, 10n26, 16, 17, 32n14
Miller, Patricia Cox, 64, 117
Mimicry, 67, 74, 77, 87, 89, 90, 90n57, 99
Mind, vi, 3, 17, 18, 20, 22, 26–28, 33–35, 37, 39, 41, 43, 45, 46, 59, 60, 64, 68, 70, 71, 77n26, 81, 84, 88, 97, 98, 98n81, 102, 103, 105, 106, 107n107, 109–113, 115, 118
Monomorphic, vi, 66n9, 72n19
Monomorphism, 66n9
Moses, 49, 54, 77n25, 85n47
Mozart, 89
Mute natures, 26, 105

N

Nestorians, 12, 17, 32
Nightingale, 75, 76n24

O

Ovid, 74

P

Parrot, v, vi, ix, 2–4, 7–9, 7n19, 9n23, 11, 13–16, 18, 19, 20n34, 21–23, 26, 30, 33, 37, 64, 65, 66n9, 67–76, 70n17, 75n21, 76n24, 78, 78n28, 79, 79n29, 80n30, 80n31, 81, 82n36, 82n38, 83–118, 84n44, 86n49, 86n50, 87n53, 89n54, 90n57, 90n59, 91n60, 91n61, 93n66, 98n81, 98n83, 99n85, 103n94, 104n96, 107n106, 107n107, 107n108, 112n122, 115n125, 115n126, 116n129, 116n130, 116n131, 117n133
Parrot religion, 67
Pedagogy, 88, 89, 91–93
Pen, 15, 26, 68, 105, 112
Performance studies, v
Peter the Fuller, 2, 4, 7–10, 10n26, 70n17, 76
Petronius, 74

Philoxenos, 3, 10, 10n26, 14, 15n33, 17
Philoxenus of Mabbug, 14n31, 115, 115n125
Pliny, 89, 92
Plutarch, 65, 80
Poll, 100, 100n87, 101
Porphyry, 65
Pronouns, vi

Q
Quaternity, 15, 15n33, 16, 29, 97
Queneau, Raymond, 109, 111

R
Reed, Morgan, 5
Religion, 68, 84–87, 85n46, 85n47, 107, 109
Rēmzā, 14, 18, 23, 28n6, 37, 38n33
Revelation, 19, 22, 42, 68, 74, 88, 107, 108, 112, 115n125, 117, 118

S
St. Peter's, Antioch, 11, 16, 37n31, 69, 69n16, 105, 112, 113
Satan, vi, 10, 16, 18, 20, 29, 30, 36, 44, 45, 54, 59, 70, 113
Seraphim, 31, 40, 42, 71–73, 76, 96, 113, 117
Serres, Michel, 64n1, 65, 68, 82, 82n39, 83, 106, 106n104
Sign, 14, 18, 19, 23, 26, 28, 34, 35, 37–39, 69, 71, 72, 88, 102, 105, 114, 118
Sign of God, 16, 19, 23, 38, 69–71, 102
Silence, 41, 66n9, 82, 102–105, 112
Slavery, 103, 104n96

Slaves, 78, 83n41, 103, 104
Sound, 68, 102–105
Soundscape, 69n16, 113
Speech, vi, 3, 22, 40, 64, 65, 67–70, 75, 76, 79–81, 83, 84, 89, 91–93, 97–107, 107n106, 110–113, 115, 118
Spinoza, Benedict de, 98
Statius, 74
Students, 70, 72, 88, 91
Syriac, 2

T
Tannous, Jack, 5
Teacher, 26, 38, 41, 42, 69, 70, 72, 88, 94–96
Temple, William, 35, 98, 100
Theodoret of Cyrrhus, 95
Tintin, 106
Tongue, 26, 40–42, 45, 53, 69, 73, 76n24, 80, 90–92, 90n58, 112
Trinity, 3, 15, 15n33, 16, 21, 23, 29, 29n9, 57, 60
Trisagion, v, 2, 4, 9, 11, 13–17, 19–21, 31n12, 40, 64
Trumpet, 23, 44, 49, 60, 72, 74
Ṭūṭī-Nāma, (Tales of a Parrot), 86

V
van Esbroeck, Michel, 7, 7n19, 20
Vergani, Emidio, 8, 8n20
Ver-Vert, 87
Virgin Mary, 12
Voice, 3, 8, 11, 15, 16, 19, 26–31, 33, 37, 38, 40, 41, 49, 50, 56, 57, 61, 63, 65, 67, 69–73, 78, 80, 81, 83, 90n58, 91, 92, 96, 97, 100–102, 102n91, 105–107, 113, 114, 116–118
von den Steinen, Karl, 108

W
Warhol, Andy, vii, 66n9
White, Lionel, 74
Wings, 19, 26, 35, 40, 41, 55, 71, 72, 79, 83, 86, 96, 114n123, 115, 117
Wittgenstein's lion, 118

Women, 48, 66n9, 83n41, 103, 104n96
Word of God, 27

Z
Zazie dans le métro, 109

Printed by Libri Plureos GmbH
in Hamburg, Germany